AN ANNOTATED BIBLIOGRAPHY
OF THE WORK OF THE
CANON LAW SOCIETY OF AMERICA
1965-1980

by
Richard G. Cunningham, J.C.D.

Canon Law Society of America
The Catholic University of America
Washington, D.C. 20064

FOREWORD

Richard G. Cunningham, J.C.D., provides a unique service to the members of the Canon Law Society of America, other canon lawyers, scholars and the Church at large with this *Annotated Bibliography of the Work of the Canon Law Society of America 1965-1980*. The project has been several years in the making, and represents a first effort to take stock of the research and writings sponsored and occasioned by the C.L.S.A.

Looking back over the past fifteen years is to look back over a time of reform, renewal, and ferment in the Catholic Church. Stimulated to a great degree by the Second Vatican Council and the currents of thought occasioned by it, the past decade and half may well prove to be one of the significant turning points in Church life, a transition which our successors will consider a milestone in the history of the Catholic Church. Living through such a period, it is difficult to discern all those elements which future generations will catalogue and critique. But it is still possible even now to appreciate these times as unusual, exciting, and of more than passing interest.

The publication of an *Annotated Bibliography* is not intended to signal the closure of a time of creative work by canon lawyers or leadership by the Canon Law Society of America. It is, instead, a taking stock of what we have attempted to date, an inventory of our efforts (whether successful or not) in order to focus our projects for the future and to steward our resources wisely.

Father Cunningham's careful labors provide canon lawyers of today and the future with an instrument of work which will enable us to build on the past without having to repeat it. As he indicates in the *Introduction*, this first effort is admittedly only a beginning. Readers are encouraged to contact him with corrections, additions or other comments in view of possible future editions of this work. As we approach the promulgation of a revised Code, it is not unlikely a new bibliography will be neded to cover a period shorter than the fifteen years represented here.

It has been a privilege to work with Father Cunningham in the preparation of this volume. I trust the service it will provide to its readers will be the source of greatest thanks we can all give to him for a work well done.

James H. Provost
Executive-Coordinator
Canon Law Society of America

INTRODUCTION

It began in the form of a mild protest. In 1963 the Canon Law Society of America was beginning its twenty-fifth year. At the New York Convention some members appeared restless, dissatisfied with what they viewed as the Society's traditional internal mode of operation. They believed that the CLSA since its inception had had only a minimal external effect on the Church as a whole. They were convinced that the time had come to move beyond what they perceived as the Society's private needs.

Pope John XXIII had called for a revision of the Code of Canon Law. Vatican II was in its second session. An awareness of *aggiornamento* challenged the Church. A growing number of American canonists saw the mid-sixties as a time for a new spirit of responsibility, a collegiate responsibility to the whole Church, a time for the CLSA to set into motion a positive plan that would contribute to the world-wide process of revision.

This small seed of discontent grew rapidly, flourishing into a substantial, dynamic body which arrived in San Francisco in 1964 to herald the start of a new and vital era. In a departure from the past the official slate of officers offered by the Nominations Committee was rejected and a majority group of members nominated and elected from the floor their own candidates.

Adding substance to this symbol, a new constitution, based on suggestions solicited from the entire membership, was adopted. Built on the promotion of canonical reform and education, the CLSA offered its assistance to the Church in its pastoral ministry. Cooperation with individuals and organizations doing research in the other sacred sciences was introduced and the Society committed itself to the service of the hierarchy on canonical matters with the pledge to participate in the constant renewal of the law by canonical research and proposals for revision.

Much of the toil of the CLSA in the years that followed (1965-1980) is represented in the contents of this work. Over 200 authors, more than double that amount of articles, eight major symposia, dozens of publications, seminars and workshops demonstrate vividly the effort and the effect that the men and women of the Canon Law Society of America have contributed to a variety of areas. Due proces, the renewal of religious life, Church ministry, the selection of bishops, the status of women, juridical procedures in tribunals, the American Procecdural Norms, the revision of the Code of Canon Law, the role of minorities in the Church, the theology of marriage, collaboration with Orthodox Churches and fiscal accountability represent

iv

only a part of the list.

This annotated bibliography describes and identifies the variety of labors of many persons over a fifteen year period in the post-conciliar Church. It is the result of a proposal by the CLSA's Committee on Research and Discussion, a project outline drawn up by Robert Sanson, and a request from the Board of Governors to the undersigned to carry out this project.

By reviewing a number of periodicals and other works an attempt has been made to collect in some sort of systematic manner the books, papers, workshops and symposia undertaken by members of the CLSA or under the auspices of the Soceity.

The principal entries will be found under the author's name. A brief *précis* describes the work. Subject matter entries refer the reader back to the author.

The most often used reference is *Proceedings*. This is the yearly publication *Proceedings of the Annual Convention of the Canon Law Society of America* with the particular year identified, e.g., '75 *Proceedings*.

Other works researched include *America, Canon Law Abstracts, The Canon Law Society of Great Britain and Ireland Newsletter, Chicago Studies, The Clergy Review* (London), *The Jurist, Origins,* and *Studia Canonica*. Histories of the Canon Law Society of America may be found in volumes 16 and 17 of *The New Catholic Encyclopedia.*

A word of gratitude is due to James Provost, the Executive-Coordinator of the Canon Law Society of America, for the many hours he has given to this project. His reading and editing of the text together with his research of additional materials has been immensely helpful in finalizing this Bibliography.

The undersigned, however, accepts responsibility for this compilation and the summaries of the material. In the interest of future accuracy in a project of this nature the undersigned would appreciate being notified regarding any errors in this work.

Richard G. Cunningham
St. John's Seminary
Brighton, MA 02135

ANNOTATED BIBLIOGRAPHY

-A-

Abortion, *see* Noonan, J., "Abortion on Demand as the Law of the Land."

Administrative Law, *see* Kennedy, R., "Administrative Law: New Proposed Roman Norms."

Advocate, *see* Canonist.

Agency, *see* Peter, V., "Problems of Agency and Moral Responsibility: A Practical Proposal."

Ahern, Barnabas M., "Law and the Gospel," *Law for Liberty*, 93-108.
The relationship of law and gospel is explored in the Old and New Testaments. The law maker in the Church has an ancillary role: good law depends upon good theology; law is totally dependent on the law of the Spirit. *See* CLSA Symposia, *The Role of Law in the Church.*

Albany, Tribunal of, *see* Swierzowski, S., et al., "The Use of Objective and Projective Personality Test Data in the Determination of Nullity of Marriages: A New Method."

Albuquerque, *see* CLSA, *Proceedings of the Forty-First Annual Convention*, Albuquerque, New Mexico, 1979.

Alesandro, John, "Colloquium: Notre Dame University, May 4-7, 1975," '75 *Proceedings*, 139-153.
The author reports on the CLSA's participation in an inter-organizational discussion on the state of the Church today, especially in the United States, and the outlook for the next decade. Points discussed included justice, education, identity, leadership and ministry. There were workshops on women's rights, reform of the clerical system, ministerial accountability, Black, Spanish, multi-cultural and multi-ethnic empowerment, economic and political issues, and Church government.
This colloquium was an outgrowth of the *Think Tank* sponsored by the CLSA at Douglaston, New York, May, 1974. (*See* '74 *Proceedings*, 122-129.)

"The Revision of Church Law: Conflict and Reconciliation," *The Jurist*, 40 (1980) 1-26.

In an address to the Western Regional Conference in 1979, the author draws on Lonergan's distinction between a classicist world view to historical mindedness. Alesandro applies this to procedural law, the revision of the Code, and marriage. He draws several conclusions illustrating the practical difference between the two approaches.

See B. Lonergan, "The Transition from a Classicist World View to Historical Mindedness."

See Morrisey, F., Fellhauer, D., & Alesandro, J., "Marriage Legislation in the New Code."

Alienation, *see* Conveyance.

Ament, Richard J., "People With Dignity: A Pastoral Program for the Divorced Catholic," *The Living Light*, 13 (1976) 577-581.

An associate pastor describes a plan of action to provide specialized ministry to divorced and remarried Catholics. *See* CLSA, Committee on Continuing Education.

America, *see*

Ball, W., "Law and Religion in America: The New Picture."

Hennesey, J., "The American Church and Church Law."

Kennedy, R., "The Early Republic's Challenge to Catholic Church Governance: Bicentennial Reflections of an American Canonist."

Mansfield, J., "A Bill of Rights for the Church: Relevance of the Anglo-American Experience."

American Culture, *see* Kelleher, S., "Canon 1014 and American Culture."

American Jurisprudence, *see*

Boyle, P., *American Jurisprudence*.

CLSA Publications, *Matrimonial Jurisprudence, United States*.

Maida, A., *The Tribunal Reporter*.

Wrenn, L., *Annulments*.

Wrenn, L., *Decisions*.

American Procedural Norms, Hartford, CT, CLSA, 1970.

This is a small booklet containing the norms, an unofficial commentary on them, and an index.

In 1968, through the initiative of the CLSA and the Bishops' Committee for Canonical Affairs, twenty-three procedural norms for the adjudication of cases of nullity of marriage were developed. After the approval of the NCCB, Pope Paul VI granted to the Church in the United States on July 1, 1970, permission to use these particular laws. They are known as the American Procedural Norms [APN].

The use of these norms has streamlined the procedure for handling marriage cases in the dioceses of the United States. Permission to continue the use of them was renewed in 1973 and in 1974. They remain in effect until the promulgation of a new Code of Canon Law.

The APN were instrumental in the promulgation of the *motu proprio* of Pope Paul VI, *Causas Matrimoniales*, on March 28, 1971, which document helped to expedite the handling of marriage cases throughout the world.

See also Doyle, T., & Licari, R., " 'Everything You Ever Wanted to Know About the Competent Forum But Were Afraid to Ask.' "

Green, T., "*Causas Matrimoniales* and the APN—A Survey."

LaDue, W., "*Causas Matrimoniales* and the American Procedural Norms —A Comparison."

Thrasher, R., "Reflections on Canon 1014."

Wrenn, L., *Annulments.*

Analogy of Law, *see* Bourke, V., "The Analogy of Law."

Anointing of the Sick, *see* Green, T., et al., "Reflections on Other Parts of the Proposed Draft *De Sacramentis.*"

Annulments, *see*

CLSA Publications, *Matrimonial Jurisprudence, United States.*

Green, T., "Canonical-Pastoral Reflections on Divorce and Remarriage."

Maida, A., *The Tribunal Reporter.*

Provost, J., "Tribunal Future Shock: Alternatives for Justice."

van der Poel, C., "Influences of an 'Anulment Mentality.' "

Wrenn, L., *Annulments.*

Wrenn, L., *Decisions.*

Apostolic Succession, *see* Burghardt, W., "Church Structure: A Theologian Reflects on History."

Arbitration, *see* Due Process.

Arico, Carl J., "A General Check List for Diocesan Policies on Pastoral Marriage Preparation," *Marriage Studies I*, 38-40.

> Elements to be included in a policy program, and diocesan approach to marriage preparation policies are described. Various resource persons are listed for further consultation.

Atlanta, *see* CLSA, *Proceedings of the Thirty-Third Annual Convention*, Atlanta, Georgia, 1971.

Authority, *see*

> Borgia, M.F., "The Recent Experiences in Religious Renewal."
>
> CLSA Symposia, *Co-responsibility in the Church.*
>
> Crosson, F., "Liberty and Authority in the Church."
>
> Fontinell, E., "Authority and Freedom in the Christian Community, Expressed in the Structures of the Institution."
>
> Hess, H., "Authority: Its Source, Nature and Purpose in the Church."
>
> Hess, H., "The Early Expression of Ecclesiastical Authority and Its Development."
>
> Meyendorff, J., "Historical Relativism and Authority in Christian Dogma."
>
> Murray, J.C., "Freedom, Authority, Community."
>
> O'Dea, T., "Authority and Freedom in the Church: Tension, Balance and Contradiction: An Historico-Sociological View."
>
> O'Hanlon, D., "The Nature, Extent and Style of Authority in the Church."
>
> Padovano, A., "A Theology of Church Government."
>
> Sexton, W., "A Comparative Examination of the Exercise of Authority in the Church."
>
> Swift, T., "The Human Dimensions of Authority and Obedience in a Faith Community."
>
> Warwick, D., "Personal and Organizational Effectiveness in the Roman Catholic Church."

Authority and Due Process, *see* Gumbleton, T., "Due Process in the Church."

-B-

Ball, William, "Law and Religion in America: The New Picture," 69 *Proceedings*, 78-88.

The author addresses himself to the matter of Church-State relations, illustrating the meeting of law and religion on the American scene. After offering a brief overview of American history, Ball shows how this past influences areas such as aid to education in religiously affiliated schools, the free exercise and equal protection clauses of the Constitution, censorship, and the right to life.

Baltimore, *see* Burns, D. "Committee Report on Legislation of Councils of Baltimore."

Banks, Robert, "Ecclesial Disobedience," *The Jurist*, 30 (1970) 91-102.

This paper was presented at the 1969 Eastern Regional Meeting. In it the author examines disobedience that challenges Church authorities and their decrees. Banks asks the question: whether or not there is room in the Church for a type of "Ecclesial disobedience" that would be the equivalent to civil disobedience.

A review of J. Coriden's *The Case for Freedom: Human Rights in the Church, The Jurist*, 30 (1970) 239-241.

Baptism, *see*

Bevilacqua, A., "Problem Areas in Chancery Practice."

Bevilacqua, A., "Canonical Bases for Deferral or Refusal of Baptism and Marriage."

Buckley, F., "The Rights to the Sacraments of Initiation."

Green, T., "Reflections on Other Parts of the Proposed Draft *De Sacramentis.*"

Landini, L., "Baptismal Practices in Catholic Hospitals: A Theological Reflection on Canons 752 and 750."

Baptismal Register, *see* Bevilacqua, A., "Problem Areas in Chancery Practice."

Baptized Non-Believers and Marriage, *see*

Cuenin, W., "The Marriage of Baptized Non-Believers: Questions of Faith, Sacrament and Law."

O'Rourke, J., "The Faith Required for the Privilege of the Faith Dispensation."

Bassett, William, A review of J. Biechler's *Law for Liberty, The Jurist,* 28 (1968) 108-112.

ed., *The Bond of Marriage: An Ecumenical and Interdisciplinary Study,* Notre Dame, IN, University of Notre Dame Press, 1968.

In October, 1967, the CLSA sponsored a symposium at the University of Notre Dame. Theologians, scripture scholars, historians, psychologists, sociologists, canon and civil lawyers were invited to study the question of the indissolubility of Christian marrige. The papers presented at this symposium and a statement of consensus are offered in this book to "the Church and its people for their consideration." *See* CLSA Symposia, *The Bond of Marriage.*

For a review of this work, *see* Read, D., *The Jurist* 29 (1969) 104-108.

"The Marriage of Christians: Valid Contract, Valid Sacrament?" *The Bond of Marriage,* 117-169.

Bassett explores the historical development of the canonical presupposition that the marriage contract of Christians is also a sacrament. He then sets forth various limitations of the contract-sacrament theory, and raises questions about the meaning of this position of the Church today. *See* CLSA Symposia, *The Bond of Marriage.*

"Subsidiarity, Order and Freedom in the Church," *The Once & Future Church,* 205-265.

Bassett proposes a new Church order in light of applying the principle of subsidiarity within the Catholic Church. He concludes by suggesting thirty-five practical ramifications of his study. *See,* CLSA Symposia, *Unity and Subsidiarity in the Church.*

ed. *The Choosing of Bishops,* Hartford, CT, CLSA, 1971.

In 1969, the CLSA established a special committee chaired by Raymond Goedert to study the question of the selection of bishops. This book represents a portion of their work. The authors of the various papers approach the matter from theological, historical, and canonical viewpoints offering important background material to those who wish to see a greater role given to the people of God in the selection of bishops. *See* CLSA, Committee on the Selection of Bishops.

For a review of this work, *see* Morrisey, F., *Studia Canonica,* 5 (1971) 181.

& Huizing, Peter, eds., *Celibacy in the Church,* Concilium 78, New York, NY, Herder and Herder, 1972.

Several papers from the CLSA Symposium on celibacy, held prior to the 1971 Synod of Bishops, have been updated in light of Synod discussions and are published in this Canon Law volume of *Concilium* together with studies on the symbolic value of celibacy, questions about celibacy in India and Africa, and a review of the 1971 Synod from a canonical perspective. *See* CLSA Symposia, *The Future Discipline of Priestly Celibacy.*

Bauer, Francis, "Relative Incapacity to Establish a Christian Conjugal Union," '74 *Proceedings*, 36-44.

The author traces the development of several representative personality disorders and delineates their influence on the intellect and will. Bauer explains that the incapacity to enter marriage is usually not absolute, but relative and can be understood only by an evaluation of a particular union and the actual interaction of the parties involved.

Bauer, Norman, "Intercommunion: Possibilities and Practicalities," *The Clergy Review*, 63 (1978) 426-430.

In a 1978 address to the Northwest Regional Meeting of the CLSA, Bauer examines what is legitimate and appropriate in the matter of sharing the spiritual heritage which divided Christians have in common.

"People of God Schema: Clerics—Functions versus Call," '80 *Proceedings*, 115-123.

This Seminar presents the chapters on clergy in the new Code step by step, with comments periodically.

Benson, Robert, "Election by Community and Chapter: Reflection on Co-responsibility in the Historical Church, " *The Jurist*, 31 (1971) 54-80.

The author, an historian, studies the process of episcopal elections during the Middle Ages and views a return to this process as a possible means of more effectively involving the laity in the common life of a true community. *See* CLSA Symposia, *Co-responsibility in the Church.*

Bennet, Arthur P., "The Practical Effects on the Fiscal Administration of Church Finances of Book Five: The Law Regarding Church Possessions," '80 *Proceedings*, 171-178.

Pertinent canons are commented on in view of American diocesan practice, the need for accountability and subsidiarity.

Bernadin, Joseph, "Keynote Address," (On Marriage and Family Life) '73 *Proceedings*, 1-7.

Bernadin emphasizes that the pastoral care we should give to those married, those contemplating marriage, and those whose marriages have failed must be based on sound theology. He offers specific recommendations regarding the refining and improving of procedural law and the operation of tribunals.

Berrigan, Frs. Daniel & Philip, *see* Stringfellow, W., "The Law, the Church and the Needs of Society."

Bevilacqua, Anthony, "Problem Areas in Chancery Practice," '75 *Proceedings*, 48-69.

In outline form Bevilacqua covers a potpourri of chancery problems including dispensations from the form and place of marriage, recording marriages, annotations of marriages in baptismal registers, the officiating priest, special cases, impediments of mixed religion and disparity of cult, promises, extraordinary form of marriage, proxy marriages, inter-ritual marriages, sanation of marriages, *vetitum*, priest as civil official only, civil marriages, baptismal registers, extraordinary ministers of the Eucharist, intercommunion, laicization of priests, national parishes, and alienation.

"Canonical Bases for Deferral or Refusal of Baptism and Marriage," '76 *Proceedings*, 52-73.

Also entitled "Problem Areas in Chancery Practice," this is a seminar outline in which the author discusses the specific problem areas, cautions, and evaluation of individual canonical reasons for deferring or refusing baptism or marriage.

ed. *The ERA in Debate: What Can it Mean for Church Law?* Toledo, OH, CLSA, 1978.

In 1977 the CLSA Board of Governors appointed a special Task Force, under the chairmanship of Anthony Bevilacqua, to consider the Equal Rights Amendment in relationship to its effectiveness in achieving and protecting women's rights and its impact on the Roman Catholic Church.

This work is a summary informational study of the history, meaning, and interpretation of the amendment. The impact of ERA on particular issues such as military service, employment, family, homosexuality, abortion, privacy rights, Roman Catholic Church legislation and ministry is analyzed.

Without disputing the ends of this movement the study concludes with arguments both in favor of and in opposition to a constitutional amendment as an appropriate means or vehicle for reform.

The work also contains a bibliography and an appendix listing approximately 150 canons in the present Code that differentiate between men and women.

Biechler, James, ed., *Recent Roman Replies*, Hartford, CT, CLSA, 1966.
This is a collection of decrees and decisions.

ed., "The Role of Law in the Church," *The Jurist*, 27 (1967) 163-181.
This is a statement of consensus and a summary of conclusions reached at the first CLSA sponsored symposium at Pittsburgh in October, 1966.

ed., *Law for Liberty: The Role of the Law in the Church Today*, Baltimore, MD, Helicon, 1967.
This book contains the complete papers and final consensus statements from the 1966 Pittsburgh symposium which explored the role of law in the Church. *See* CLSA Symposia, *The Role of Law in the Church.*
For a review of this work, *see* Bassett, W., *The Jurist*, 28 (1968) 108-112.

See McDonald, J. & Biechler, J., "New Horizons in Canon Law."

Bill of Rights, *see*

Mansfield, J., "A Bill of Rights for the Church: Relevance of the Anglo-American Experience."

Whelan, C., "Problems of Drafting a Bill of Rights for the Church."

Bishop, *see*

CLSA Symposia, *Co-responsibility in the Church.*

Ellis, J.T., "Those Called to Lead—Then and Now."

Heston, E., "Present Organizational Design and Structure of the Roman Catholic Church."

Moudry, J., "Bishop and Priest in the Sacrament of Holy Orders."

Nardoni, E., "Ministries in the New Testament."

Ryan, R., "The Dispensing Authority of the Residential Bishop."

Bishop, Selection of, *see*

Bassett, W., ed., *The Choosing of Bishops.*

Benson, R., "Election by Community and Chapter: Reflection on Co-Responsibility in the Historical Church."

CLSA, Committee on the Selection of Bishops.

CLSA Publications, *Provisional Plan for Choosing Bishops.*

CLSA Publications, *Procedure for the Selection of Bishops in the United States: A Suggested Implementation of Present Papal Norms.*

Goedert, R., "Selection of Bishops: A Canonical and Pastoral Critique of the New Norms."

Lynch, J., "Co-responsibility in the First Five Centuries: Presbyteral Colleges and the Election of Bishops."

Bissonnette, Rita-Mae, "Ecclesiastical Ministry and Women," '76 *Proceedings*, 107-117.

The author examines the meaning of "ministry" and the role of women in the ministry. The canonical obstacles are reviewed and possible alternatives offered. Bissonnette points out that the Church must begin with an official and public recognition of those ministries which women are, in fact, already doing.

Bissonnette, Tomas, "Comunidades Ecclesiales de Base: Some Contemporary Attempts to Build Ecclesial *Koinonia*," *The Jurist*, 36 (1976) 24-58.

The author explores the North American experience of basic ecclesial communities and notes the practical viability of the communion model of Church at the local level. *See* CLSA Permanent Seminar.

Bohr, David, "Evangelization: The Essential and Primary Mission of the Church," *The Jurist*, 39 (1979) 40-87.

After adopting a broad definition of evangelization in two stages, the author analyzes the renewed meanings of evangelization since the 1974 Synod of Bishops. Bohr then clarifies the Church's situation in the world in terms of reconciliation. *See* CLSA Permanent Seminar.

Bond of Marriage, The: An Ecumenical and Interdisciplinary Study, see Bassett, W., ed.; CLSA Symposia, *The Bond of Marriage*.

Borgia, M. Francis, "Recent Experiences in Religious Renewal," '69 *Proceedings*, 122-128.

The author examines five principles at work in the day-to-day living of the apostolic religious, viz., the dynamic of religious life, relationship, respect for person, mission, and fellowship authority. Borgia then shows how these have effected major changes in the whole manner of religious living.

Bourke, Myles, "Collegial Decision Making in the New Testament," *The Jurist*, 31 (1971) 1-13.

Scripture scholar Bourke believes that in First Corinthians and other New Testament sources suggestions can be found relating to the active role the laity is to have in the Church assembly. *See* CLSA Symposia, *Co-responsibility in the Church.*

Bourke, Vernon J., "The Analogy of Law," *Law for Liberty*, 140-146.

Exploring different approaches to definition of law, Bourke highlights the scholastic insight of analogy and applies it to several current issues in Church life. *See* CLSA Symposia, *The Role of Law in the Church.*

"Marital Fidelity and Philosophy," *Divorce and Remarriage in the Catholic Church*, 41-64.

The approach to fidelity in various contemporary philosophical systems is set forth. Bourke argues for the need of fidelity in the special interpersonal relationship which is marriage. *See* CLSA, Committee on Tribunal Decision Making.

Bowen, Henry, "Ecumenism and the Local Community," '77 *Proceedings*, 87-93.

The author offers examples and suggestions for applying the general principles of law relative to ecumenism to everyday practice.

Boyle, Paul, "The Renewal of Canon Law and the Resolutions of the Canon Law Society of America, 1965," in *Renewal and Canon Law, Concilium*, vol. 28, New York, N.Y., Paulist Press, 1967, 69-77.

The author offers reflections on the 1965 norms approved by the CLSA. These include general principles, ecumenical principles, pluralistic principles, and principles dealing with the rights and dignity of persons.

American Jurisprudence, St. Meinrad Archabbey, St. Meinrad, IN, CLSA, [no date given].

ed. *Discussions on the Motu Proprio Ecclesiae Sanctae*, Hartford, CT, CLSA, 1966.

ed. *Selected Passages from Religious Constitutions Dealing with the Evangelical Counsels and Community Life*, Hartford CT, CLSA, 1967.

Braceland, Francis, "Psychoneurotic Interpersonal Reaction: Incompatibility and the Tribunal," '70 *Proceedings*, 63-70.

The author discusses emotional incompatibility in general and the pain, distress and ineptitude which neuroses bring in their wake. After offering some specific cases, Braceland concludes with a consideration of the syndrome entitled "Search of a Mother."

Bradburn, Norman, "Reflections on the Socio-Psychological Dimensions of Leadership and Some Possible Applications to the Church," *The Jurist*, 31 (1971) 250-265.

The author examines the leadership crisis in the Church today from the point of view of a social-psychologist and he applies to the Church examples of contemporary theories of organization and leadership. *See* CLSA Symposia, *Co-responsibility in the Church.*

Brennan, Margaret, "Standing in Experience: A Reflection on the Status of Women in the Church," '75 *Proceedings*, 12-25. (*Also, Origins*, v. 5, 295-299.)

The author presents a summary of the central ideas that are becoming more and more a part of the consciousness of many American religious women. Brennan offers insights and implications on experience and law in the American context and how this dynamic is presently at work within the lives of American religious women in terms of both apostolic and contemplative communities. She concludes with a call to canon lawyers to the original idea of Church as that of many members in which all are partners in the work of Jesus Christ and all must be free to serve the Lord and His people.

Bridston, Keith, "The Polity and Politics of Church Unity," *We, The People of God . . .* , 173-182.

Bridston, a Lutheran theologian, explores the differences between Roman Catholics and Lutherans to find a similarity of polity but difficulties in politics in reaching Church unity. *See* CLSA Symposia, *A Constitution for the Church.*

Brossard, André, "Role of the Advocate in the Development of Jurisprudence," '74 *Proceedings*, 106-108.

This is a brief outline of a seminar.

Brown, Earl Kent, "Co-responsibility in Church Governance: Some Protestant Experiences," *The Jurist*, 31 (1971) 187-222.

The author, a church historian, discusses congregationalism, preseby-terianism and episcopalianism, and the participation of the laity in each communion. Brown concludes with a review of the plan entitled "The Consultation on Church Union." *See* CLSA Symposia, *Co-responsibility in the Church.*

Brown, Ralph, The Development of Local Jurisprudence," '69 *Proceedings*, 52-55.

The author speaks of the parallel work in the United States and Great Britain of publishing the decisions of marrige tribunals. He cites some specific examples which indicate the need of close attention on a local basis to our own jurisprudence, as well as that of the Rota, as guidelines in the process of decision making. Brown believes that by a cross sharing of local jurisprudence a kind of anglo-saxon jurisprudence will grow up and this is a contribution that we as canon lawyers can make to the service of our fellows and the growth of the Church.

"Non-inclusion: A Form of Simulation," '79 *Proceedings*, 1-11.

Brown analyzes the presumption that persons entering marriage intend to be in accord with what the Church teaches about marriage. He studies the implications of this presumption not being born out, especially in the areas of non-inclusion of children, permanency and fidelity. After examining simple error and implicit intention, he suggests a simpler approach to the question of simulation.

Brundage, James, "The Creative Canonist: His Role in Church Reform," '70 *Proceedings*, 15-28. (*Also, The Jurist*, 31 (1971) 301-318.)

The author suggests that canonists have a responsibility to play a larger creative role than they have commonly done during the past half-century in the process of applying the law of the Church to concrete human situations. He offers three basic kinds of innovation drawn from the classical period; viz., limiting the application of legislation, creating new law and new legal positions by advancing solutions to problems which no legislator has dealt with, and adapting existing legal mechanisms to deal with problems for which the original mechanisms were never designed. Brundage concludes with specific recommendations for substantially modifying the structure of the proposed new Code, stating, "the Church and the salvation of souls . . . have been best served when her canon lawyers have vigorously and imaginatively exercised their creative role."

Brunett, Alex, "The Diocesan Synod of Detroit: The Theology Underlying the Synod Document," '69 *Proceedings*, 112-115.

Brunett explains how this Synod was a response in faith to God of all the Catholics of the Archdiocese of Detroit as an expression of their covenant—a sacred pledge between the bishop and the faithful, the community and Christ, Christ and the Father—in order to witness to all that they are Christians.

Buckley, Francis, "The Right to the Sacraments of Initiation," '78 *Proceedings*, 60-73. (*Also, Origins*, v. 8, 329-336.)

The author studies the sacraments of initiation as actions of the Church in expressing and celebrating the presence and action of God in the midst of His people. Buckley includes infant and adult baptism, confirmation and first communion as well as inter-communion in his discussion.

Buckley, John & Schmidt, Ronald, "Experience and Possibilities of Canonical Legal Aid," '70 *Proceedings*, 88-90.

> The authors explain how the idea of establishing a kind of canonical legal aid society grew out of the experiences of the Committee of Concerned Canon Lawyers who assisted the nineteen Washington priests in their difficulties with Cardinal O'Boyle. A recommendation is made that such a committee be set up by the CLSA on a permanent basis.

Burghardt, Walter, "Church Structure: A Theologian Reflects on History," '71 *Proceedings*, 11-22.

> The author examines certain assumptions, viz., apostolic succession, ministerial priesthood and non-historical orthodoxy (vs. historical consciousness). Burghardt views these matters as obstacles to true reform in the Church.

Burns, Dennis, "Moral Certitude," '75 *Proceedings*, 38-47.

> The author examines moral certitude as the basis for judging the validity or invalidity of a marriage. Burns uses for his study some papal allocutions, various studies, and Rotal jurisprudence.

"Report on Privilege of the Faith Cases," '76 *Proceedings*, 167-182.

> This is a study and a survey on the matter of Roman requirements and procedures in the handling of Privilege of the Faith cases.

"Procedure in Second Instance Courts," '77 *Proceedings*, 112-130.

> This is a seminar on a survey study of present and potential caseloads, the procedures that are used and the problems that are experienced.

et al., "Committee Report on Legislation of Councils of Baltimore," '69 *Proceedings*, 132-142.

> The NCCB requested a study of the legislation of the Plenary Councils of Baltimore in order to determine what laws were still in force *de jure* and what should be done in these matters *de facto*.

> The CLSA Committee, chaired by Dennis Burns, concludes that the remaining conciliar legislation be abrogated and that the matters involved therein be left to the direction of the Code of Canon Law.

et al., "Report of Committee for Tribunal Assistance, " '73 *Proceedings*, 138-147.

> A national survey undertaken by this CLSA committee, chaired by Dennis Burns, indicates that the present status of American Tribunals is "creaking." Conclusions and recommendations are offered to improve the situation.

& Griffin, Bertram, "Tribunal Procedure" '72 *Proceedings*, 76-82.
This seminar, co-chaired by Dennis Burns and Bertram Griffin, was offered as an aid for tribunals limited in personnel, resources, and training. Three practical forms are discussed, viz., the "Frontier" Tribunal, Regional Tribunals, and Diocesan Circuit Courts.

-C-

Cain, James, "The Chancery in a Changing Church, " '78 *Proceedings*, 34-37.
The author expresses his belief that the meaning of "chancery" in the post-Vatican II Church suggests that it coordinate pastoral planning by promotion, facilitation, and implementation.

Canon Law and Dogma, *see* Pelikan, J., "Law and Dogma: Some Historical Interrelations."

Canon Law, Pastoral Guide to, *see* CLSA, Committee on Continuing Education.

Canon Law, Teaching, *see*

Golden, P., "Teaching Canon Law."

Golden, P. & Green, T., "Teaching Canon Law Today."

Golden, P. & Hill, R., "Report on Survey of Teachers of Canon Law."

Lonsway, F., "The Case Study Method of Teaching Canon Law."

Canon Law Society of America, *see* CLSA.

Canonical Legal Aid Society, *see* Buckley, J. & Schmidt, R., "Experience and Possibilities of Canonical Legal Aid."

Canonical Significance of Papal and Curial Pronouncements, see Morrisey, F.

Canonist, *see*

Brossard, A., "Role of the Advocate in the Development of Jurisprudence."

Brundage, J., "The Creative Canonist: His Role on Church Reform."

Francis, J., "The Canonists—Advocate."

Kennedy, R., "The Early Republic's Challenge to Catholic Church Governance: Bicentennial Reflections of an American Canonist."

Maida, A., "Visionary or Reactionary: The Canonist's Challenge to Create."

McManus, F., "Role of the Canonist: Interpreter and Advocate."

O'Malley, P., "The Canon Law Society of America and the Needs of the Ministry."

Sheets, J., "Ministry, Spirituality and the Canon Lawyer."

Cardman, Francine, "Tradition, Hermeneutics and Ordination," *Sexism and Church Law*, 58-81.

Contemporary approaches to hermeneutics, or the science of interpretation, are applied to the tradition of the Church which prohibits the ordination of women, in order to come to a clearer understanding of how binding that tradition may be. *See* CLSA Symposia, *Women and Church Law.*

Carey, Raymond, "The Good Faith Solution," *The Jurist*, 29 (1969) 428-438.

This paper was presented at the Midwest Canon Law Workshop at Chicago in 1968 and addresses the practice of the Chicago Tribunal in the handling of marriage cases that are not capable of canonical disposition. Positive and negative arguments are offered in regard to the procedure and several questions are posed for discussion.

Cargill, Joan, "Understanding the One-Parent Child in the Classroom," *The Living Light*, 13 (1976) 599-600.

A teacher reflects on the difficulties of an understanding approach to children of divorce in the classroom setting. *See* CLSA, Committee on Continuing Education.

Carney, Richard, "New Applications of Canon 1127," '77 *Proceedings*, 49-52.

The author investigates the worth and value of resolving doubtfully valid marriages under c. 1127, in favor of the faith, rather than in favor of the marriage. This is a reversal of the presumption of law normally prescribed by c. 1014. Carney believes that c. 1127 has been too often ignored, for it can be employed in an administrative way by the Ordinary issuing a "document of liberty."

For a refutation of Carney's argument, *see* Orsy, L., "An Evaluation of 'New Applications of Canon 1127.' "

Case for Freedom, The: Human Rights in the Church, see CLSA Symposia, *Rights in the Church*; Coriden, J., ed.

Catoir, John, "An Analysis of the Evolution of Tribunal Practice," '73 *Proceedings*, 17-21.
This is a brief overview of the evolution, reasons and future of ecclesiastical tribunals.

Causas Matrimoniales, see

Green, T., "*Causas Matrimoniales* and the A.P.N.—A Survey."

LaDue, W., "*Causas Matrimoniales* and the American Procedural Norms —A Comparison."

Wrenn, L. *Annulments.*

Cautiones, see Bevilacqua, A., "Problem Areas in Chancery Practice."

Celibacy, *see*

CLSA, "Dispensed Priests in Ecclesial Ministry: A Canonical Reflection."

CLSA Symposia, *The Future Discipline of Priestly Celibacy.*

Celibacy in the Church, see Bassett, W., and Huizing, P., eds.; CLSA Symposia, *The Future Discipline of Priestly Celibacy.*

Chancery, *see*

Bevilacqua, A., "Canonical Bases for Deferral or Refusal of Baptism and Marriage."

Bevilacqua, A., "Problem Areas in Chancery Practice."

Cain, J., "The Chancery in a Changing Church."

Morrissey, M., "Issues in Chancery Practice."

Chicago, Archdiocese of, *see*

Carey, R., "The Good Faith Solution."

Lucas, J., "The Role of the Tribunal in Second Marriages: The Prohibition."

Chicago Studies, see CLSA Committee on Continuing Education.

Children of Divorce, *see*

Cargill, J., "Understanding the One-Parent Child in the Classroom."

Young, J., "The Religious Educator and the Children of Divorce."

Kennedy, R., "The Early Republic's Challenge to Catholic Church Governance: Bicentennial Reflections of an American Canonist."

Kennedy, R., "Introductory Address."

Maida, A., "Visionary or Reactionary: The Canonist's Challenge to Create."

Mallett, J., "Diocesan Structure and Governance."

Padovano, A., "A Theology of Church Government."

Sheehan, M., " 'Is There Any Life in the Church Beyond the Diocese?' Supra-Diocesan Structures and Church Governance."

Thomas, B., "Models of Governance for Religious."

Church Leadership, *see*

Bradburn, N., "Reflections on the Socio-Psychological Dimensions of Leadership and Some Possible Applications to the Church."

CLSA Symposia, *Co-responsibility in the Church.*

Dillon, R., "Theory and Norms of the Governing Ministry Derived from the Gospel of St. Matthew."

Dreher, J., "New Wineskins for New Wine. The Need for Pastoral Planning and Leadership Development for a Church in Transition."

Greeley, A., "Leadership and Friendship: A Sociologist's Viewpoint."

Church Mission, *see*

CLSA Permanent Seminar, and its results published in *The Jurist*, 39 (1979) 1-288.

Hehir, J., "The Church in Misson: Canonical Implications."

Church Reform, *see* Brundage, J., "The Creative Canonist: His Role in Church Reform."

Church-State Relations, *see*

Ball, W., "Law and Religion in America: The New Picture."

Hennesey, J., "Papal Diplomacy and the Contemporary Church."

Church Structure, *see*

Burghardt, W., "Church Structure: A Theologian Reflects on History."

Fontinell, E., "Authority and Freedom in the Christian Community, Expressed in the Structures of the Institution."

Heston, E., "Present Organizational Design and Structure of the Roman Catholic Church."

Mallet, J., "Diocesan Structure and Governance."

Provost, J., "Structuring the Church as *Communio.*"

Provost, J., "Structuring the Church as *Missio.*"

Provost, J., "Structuring the Community."

Sheehan, M., " 'Is There Any Life in the Church Beyond the Diocese?' Supra-Diocesan Structures and Church Governance."

Classicist World-View, *see*

Alesandro, J., "The Revision of Church Law: Conflict and Reconciliation."

Lonergan, B., "The Transition from a Classicist World-View to Historical Mindedness."

Clergy, *see*

Bauer, N., "People of God Schema: Clerics—Function versus Call."

Warwick, D., "Personal and Organizational Effectiveness in the Roman Catholic Church."

Cleveland, *see* CLSA, *Proceedings of the Thirty-First Annual Convention,* Cleveland, Ohio, 1969.

CLSA, "Code of Professional Responsibility," '79 *Proceedings,* 136-145. (*Also, The Jurist,* 39 [1979] 487-493.)

CLSA Committee on Alternatives to Tribunal Procedures, "Statement," '75 *Proceedings,* 162-178. (*Also, Origins,* v. 5, 273-285.)

This is also referred to as "The McDevitt Report." *See* McDevitt, A.

CLSA Committee on Continuing Education.

This committee was established as a result of the Think Tank (q.v.) in an effort to make available to a broader public the research being done by the CLSA and developments within Church law. Three major projects were completed by the committee under the chair of Patrick Collins. A series of articles in question and answer format were produced as "The Pastoral Guide to Canon Law," *Chicago Studies,* 15 (1976) no. 3. A special feature was developed for religious educators, "Ministry to Separated, Divorced and Remarried Catholics," *The Living Light,* 13 (1976) 545-611. Materials including video-tapes, film strip, leader's guide, scripts and background paper were developed to assist in programs for continuing education of clergy; *see* CLSA Publications, *Audio-Visual Learning on Marriage, Divorce, Tribunal Practice.*

CLSA Committee on Marriage Research

In 1972 the CLSA adopted a motion "to undertake and stimulate research into Christian Marriage." A committee was eventually established, and its initial results were reported by Richard Cunningham at the 1976 convention—*see* Cunningham, R., "Recent Rotal Decisions and Today's Marriage Theology: Nothing Has Changed—Or Has It?" The committee continued to survey developments in American theologians and made a progress report at the Eastern Regional meeting in 1977 but made no further reports to the national Society.

In 1973 the CLSA established a committee to investigate alternatives to tribunals. This committee reported to the annual meeting in 1975—*see* McDevitt, A., "Report of Committee on Alternatives to Tribunal Procedures." The committee was mandated at that meeting to study the canonical institute of dissolution in hopes of resolving several related issues. In 1977 the committee reported it could not do the task in its present structure, and at its recommendation a Research Director was sought to conduct the study.

In 1978 the Board of Governors combined the research mandated to the Committee on Alternatives to Tribunal Procedures and the tasks assigned the Committee on the Theology of Marriage, forming a Committee on Marriage Research and putting it under the direction of a Research Director, Thomas P. Doyle. The first results of the new effort were published in 1980—*see* Doyle, T., *Marriage Studies I.*

CLSA Committee on the Selection of Bishops.

In 1979 the National Convention adopted a resolution authorizing the Board of Governors to establish a special committee to study the question of the selection of bishops. The committee has produced three reports.

Bassett, W., ed., *The Choosing of Bishops*, Hartford, CT, CLSA, 1971.

CLSA Publications, *Provisional Plan for Choosing Bishops*, Hartford, CT, CLSA, 1971.

CLSA Publications, *Procedure for the Selection of Bishops in the United States: A Suggested Implementation of Present Papal Norms*, Hartford, CT, CLSA, 1973.

CLSA Committee on Tribunal Decision Making.

This was established at the 1970 convention in New Orleans, and resulted in the publication of an interdisciplinary study on the underlying presupposition to tribunals—namely that marriage is indissoluble. It was published, edited by its chairperson, Lawrence G. Wrenn, under the title: *Divorce and Remarriage in the Catholic Church*, New York, Newman, 1973.

CLSA, "Dispensed Priests in Ecclesial Ministry: A Canonical Reflection," *Chicago Studies*, 14 (1975) 121-133.

J. Provost, K. Lasch and H. Skillin, an *ad hoc* committee of the CLSA, analyze the law and the situation relative to priests who have been laicized. They conclude that the dispensed priest is a lay person in good standing in the Church and as such may be and is called to exercise those ministries that can be exercised by the laity and, with discretion, may be hired for any position in the Church.

CLSA, History of, *see*

Lynch, J., "Canon Law Society of America."

Heintschel, D., "Canon Law Society of America."

CLSA and the Needs of the Ministry, *see* O'Malley, P.

CLSA Permanent Seminar.

As the result of a Think Tank conducted by the CLSA in May, 1974 a Permanent Seminar was established to research fundmental issues of theology and canon law. The Permanent Seminar's first project was to examine a workable model of the Church, rooted in Christian tradition and capable of providing a vehicle for continued renewal of the Church over the next twenty-five years or more.

The results of the Permanent Seminar's initial scholarly analysis under the direction of J. Provost may be found in *The Jurist*, 36 (1976) 1-245. It is called "Church as Communion." The model selected by the Permanent Seminar Committee perceives the Church as a communion of divine life with humanity, lived in faith and expressed in community.

The second project of the Permanent Seminar complements the first. Entitled "Church as Mission," it looks to the purpose, the *raison d'être* of the Church. Papers from the seminar are published in *The Jurist*, 39 (1979), 1-288.

CLSA Publications

American Jurisprudence, Boyle, P., St. Meinrad Archabbey, St. Meinrad, IN, CLSA, [no date given].

American Procedural Norms, Hartford, CT, CLSA, 1970. (*See* American Procedural Norms.)

Annulments, Wrenn, L., Hartford, CT, CLSA, 1970; 2nd ed. 1972; 3rd ed. Toledo, OH, CLSA, 1978.

Audio-Visual Learning on Marriage, Divorce, Tribunal Practice, Hartford, CT, CLSA, 1976.

This program contains a filmstrip entitled "The Church and Marital Breakdown," with a cassette tape, reading script and historical overview. There are also five audio-visual video cassette tapes and a teaching guide available for rental. The program was developed by the CLSA Committee on Continuing Education.

Canonical Significance of Papal and Curial Pronouncements, Morrisey, F., Hartford, CT, CLSA, 1974.

Choosing of Bishops, The, Bassett, W., ed., Hartford, CT, CLSA, 1971. (*See* Bassett, W.)

"The Church and Marital Breakdown," *see above, Audio Visual Learning on Marriage, Divorce, Tribunal Practice.*

Common Sources of Nullity, Wrenn, L., ed., Hartford, CT, CLSA, 1968.

Critique of the Proposed Schemata, Hartford, CT, CLSA [no date given].

Decisions, Wrenn, L., Toledo, OH, CLSA, 1980. (*See* Wrenn, L.)

Discussions on the MOTU PROPRIO ECCLESIAE SANCTAE, Boyle, P., ed., Hartford, CT, CLSA, 1966.

ERA in Debate: What Can It Mean for Church Law? The, Bevilacqua, A., ed., Toledo, OH, CLSA, 1978.

Marriage Studies: Reflections in Canon Law and Theology, Doyle, T., ed., v. 1, Toledo, OH, CLSA, 1980. (*See* Doyle, T.)

Matrimonial Jurisprudence, United States, [no city given], CLSA v. 1, 1968-1971, Dolciamore, J., ed., 1973; v. 2, 1972, Dillon E., ed., 1974; v. 3, 1973, Schumacher, W., ed., 1975; v. 4, 1974, Stocker T., ed., 1976; v. 5, 1975-76, Stocker, T., ed., 1977.

Newsletter, CLSA.

A periodic publication for members of the Society.

On Due Process, Hartford, CT, CLSA, 1970.

This CLSA sponsored plan for due process was approved by the NCCB in November, 1969, and received a *nihil obstat* from Pope Paul VI on October 23, 1971. It has served as the springboard for the newly proposed law creating administrative tribunals in the universal Church. This is also referred to in some literature as "*Nihil Obstat* for Due Process." *See The Jurist*, 32 (1972) 291-292.

Procedure for the Selection of Bishops in the United States: A Suggested Implementation of Present Papal Norms, Hartford, CT, CLSA, 1973.

In response to the central theme of Vatican II, co-responsibility, and the widespread yearning for more participation in the choice of Church leaders, the CLSA instituted a committee in October, 1969, to study the selection of bishops.

An interdisciplinary report was published in 1971, entitled *The Choosing of Bishops*, Bassett, W., ed. It stated that no theological or canonical reasons stood in the way of a more active role on the part of the Christian community in the process of choosing bishops.

The Committee then set out to devise a practical plan whereby the entire local church would have a voice in nominating candidates.

On March 25, 1972, the Holy See issued *Episcoporum Delectum*, a set of norms to be used in the Latin Church for the appointment of bishops. These somewhat modified the existing procedures.

Finally, in March, 1973, after 3½ years of careful canonical and pastoral research and discussion, the CLSA published this work which offered to the American Church for its consideration a model for the implementation of the papal norms as well as to provide an effective procedure at the local level to carry out the principles of consultation that they embody.

Proceedings of the Canon Law Society of America.

The Thirty-First Annual Convention, Cleveland, Ohio, 1969.

The Thirty-Second Annual Convention, New Orleans, Lousiana, 1970.

The Thirty-Third Annual Convention, Atlanta Georgia, 1971.

The Thirty-Fourth Annual Convention, Seattle, Washington, 1972.

The Thirty-Fifth Annual Convention, Washington, D.C., 1973.

The Thirty-Sixth Annual Convention, St. Paul, Minnesota, 1974.

The Thirty-Seventh Annual Convention, San Diego, California, 1975. (*See* review by McManus, F., *The Jurist*, 36 [1976] 260-261.)

The Thirty-Eighth Annual Convention, Philadelphia, Pennsylvania, 1976.

The Thirty-Ninth Annual Convention, Houston, Texas, 1977.

The Fortieth Annual Convention, St. Louis, Missouri, 1978.

The Forty-First Annual Convention, Albuquerque, New Mexico, 1979.

The Forty-Second Annual Convention, Orlando, Florida, 1980.

(The minutes of the annual meetings prior to 1969 are recorded in *The Jurist.*)

Provisional Plan for Choosing Bishops, Hartford, CT, CLSA, 1971. (*Also, Origins*, v. 2, 3f.)

Renewal Through Community and Experimentation, O'Rourke, K., ed., Hartford, CT, CLSA, 1968. (*See* CLSA Workshop on *Community Life and Experimentation*.)

Selected Passages from Religious Constitutions Dealing with the Evangelical Counsels and Community Life, Boyle, P., ed., Hartford, CT, CLSA, 1967.

Simplification of Procedures in Privilege of Faith and Lack of Form Cases, Hartford, CT, CLSA, 1967.

Trullo Cases, Hartford CT, CLSA, 1975.

Who Decides for the Church? Coriden, J., ed., Hartford, CT, CLSA, 1971 (*See* CLSA Symposia, *Co-responsibility in the Church*.)

CLSA and Religious

The Society offered commentaries on *Perfectae Caritatis* (Vatican II's decree on Religious Life), together with workshops, seminars and institutes over a five-year period in order to offer positive guidance to religious communities in their renewal assemblies which were mandated by the Second Vatican Council. *See* Institutes of Life.

CLSA Resolutions

Chronicle of the Twenty-Sixth Annual Meeting, San Francisco, 1964, *The Jurist*, 25 (1965) 122-127.

Chronicle of the Twenty-Seventh Annual Meeting, Chicago, 1965, C. Bastnagel, ed., *The Jurist*, 26 (1966) 119-126.

Resolutions on Renewal of Canon Law, *The Jurist*, 26 (1966) 165-166.

Recommendations are offered for a substantial renewal of Canon Law which requires a radical reappraisal of the rights and responsibilities of institutions and individuals in the modern world. Cf. Boyle, P., "The Renewal of Canon Law and the Resolutions of the Canon Law Society of America, 1965."

Chronicle of the Twenty-Eighth Annual Meeting, Pittsburgh, 1966, C. Bastnagel, ed., *The Jurist*, 27 (1967) 139-143.

Chronicle of the Twenty-Ninth Annual Meeting, Denver, 1967, T. Swift, ed., *The Jurist*, 28 (1968) 249-261.

Resolutions of the Thirtieth Annual Meeting, Boston, 1968, *The Jurist*, 29 (1969) 26-28.

Resolutions of the Thirty-First Annual Convention, Cleveland, 1969, *The Jurist*, 30 (1970) 380-386. (*Also,* '69 *Proceedings.*)

Resolutions of the Thirty-Second Annual Convention, New Orleans, 1970, *The Jurist*, 31 (1971) 363-367. (*Also,* '70 *Proceedings.*)

Resolutions of the Thirty-Third Annual Convention, Atlanta, 1971, '71 *Proceedings.*

Resolutions of the Thirty-Fourth Annual Convention, Seattle, 1972, *The Jurist*, 32 (1972) 539-543. (*Also,* '72 *Proceedings.*)

Resolutions of the Thirty-Fifth Annual Convention, Washington, D.C., 1973, *The Jurist*, 34 (1974) 161-167. (*Also,* '73 *Proceedings.*)

Resolutions of the Thirty-Sixth Annual Convention, St. Paul, 1974, *The Jurist*, 35 (1975) 335-342. (*Also,* '74 *Proceedings.*)

Subsequent resolutions may be found in the individual volumes of *Proceedings*, 1975-1980.

CLSA Role of Law Award.

Instituted in 1973, this award is an annual honor bestowed on an individual who best exemplifies the fulfillment of the expressed ideals, goals and purposes of the CLSA. These include pastoral attitude, commitment to research and study, participation in the revision of law, response to needs and practical assistance, and facilitation of dialogue and the interchange of ideas within the Society and with other groups.

The recipients have been:

Rev. Frederick R. McManus—1973
Very Rev. Paul M. Boyle, C.P.—1974
Rev. Raymond E. Goedert—1975
Rev. Lawrence G. Wrenn—1976
Rev. Robert T. Kennedy—1977
Dr. Stephan G. Kuttner—1978
Rev. Kevin D. O'Rourke, O.P.—1979
Rev. Thomas J. Lynch—1980.

CLSA, "Statement Concerning the Revision of the Code of Canon Law, A," '77 *Proceedings*, 167-174. (*Also, The Jurist*, 38 [1978] 209-216, and *Origins*, v. 7, 337-340.)

This statement, from the 1977 Annual Convention at Houston, declares that the drafts of the new Code are unacceptable in their very substance. Appended in *The Jurist* articles are the resolutions from the 1975, 1970, 1969 and 1968 conventions.

See Harman F., "Statement by the CLSA on the Revision of the Code and Commentary." (Harman agrees with the CLSA criticisms but not with its proposals.)

See also Hill, R., "Canon Law after Vatican II: Renewal or Retreat."

CLSA Symposia.

The Role of Law in the Church.

The first CLSA sponsored symposium was held in October, 1966, at Pittsburgh. Thirty-five Christian scholars representing the fields of Scripture, Theology, Philosophy, History, Sociology and Law met to reflect on the role and function of law in the Church and to recommend the direction and content that the revision of the Code should take.

For a summary of the conclusions reached, *see The Jurist*, 27 (1967) 163-181.

For the complete papers and final consensus statement, *see* Biechler, J., ed., *Law for Liberty: The Role of Law in the Church Today*, Baltimore, MD, Helicon, 1967.

For a review of this work, *see* Bassett, W., *The Jurist*, 28 (1968) 108-112.

A Constitution for the Church.

The second symposium sponsored by the CLSA and Fordham University and funded by Our Sunday Visitor Foundation was held in October, 1967, at New York.

The position papers of the participants and the results of their proposed applications of constitutionalism to Church government were published. *See* Coriden, J., ed., *We, the People of God . . . A Study of Constitutional Government for the Church*, Huntington, IN, Our Sunday Visitor, Inc., 1968.

For a review of this work, *see* Orsy, L., *The Jurist*, 29 (1969) 210-215.

The Bond of Marriage.

A third symposium, also held in October, 1967, met at Notre Dame. It was sponsored by the CLSA in affiliation with the University of Notre Dame.

Theologians, scripture scholars, historians, canonists, civil lawyers, psychologists and sociologists studied the question of the indissolubility of marriage. For a summary of the conclusions reached, *see The Jurist*, 28 (1968) 70-73.

This symposium agreed that the present processes for annulments and dissolution of marriages are clearly inadequate for the needs of the faithful. It is suggested that the preponderance of evidence should serve as a basis for judging the existence of the marriage bond. Greater emphasis on safeguarding the dignity and rights of persons is called for, as is the solution of all marriage cases on the local level with the right of appeal being maintained.

For the complete papers and final consensus statement, *see* Basett, W., ed., *The Bond of Marriage: An Ecumenical and Interdisciplinary Study*, Notre Dame, IN, University of Notre Dame Press, 1968.

For review of this symposium, *see* Huizing, P., "The Indissolubility of Marriage and Church Order."

For a review of Bassett's work, *see* Read, D., *The Jurist*, 29 (1969) 104-108.

Rights in the Church.

The fourth symposium was held in October, 1968 at Washington. It was co-sponsored by the CLSA and the School of Canon Law of the Catholic University of America.

For a summary statement affirming the inalienable and inviolable rights and freedoms of persons in the Christian community, *see* "Towards a Declaration of Christian Freedom," *The Jurist*, 29 (1969) 1-9.

For the complete background papers and the final statement of consensus, *see* Coriden, J., ed., *The Case for Freedom: Human Rights in the Church*, Washington, D.C., Corpus Books, 1969.

For a review of this work, *see* Banks, R., *The Jurist*, 30 (1970) 239-241.

Unity and Subsidiarity in the Church: Rome and the Conference of Bishops.

The fifth symposium was co-sponsored by the CLSA and the University of Dayton with financial assistance from Our Sunday Visitor Foundation. It met in September, 1969, at Bergamo, the John XXIII Center for Renewal, Dayton, Ohio.

This symposium was an interdisciplinary study of the relations and communications between the Holy See and the National Episcopal Conferences in preparation for the Synod of Bishops held in October, 1969, at Rome.

For the position paper "Unity and Subsidiarity in the Church: Rome and the Conferences of Bishops," *see The Jurist*, 30 (1970) 85-89.

This position paper was sent to each participant in the Second World Synod of Bishops. More than fifty of the bishops requested the scholarly studies that had served as the context of this symposium. The basic suggestions of the final position paper and the thirteen propositions voted by the Synod in October, 1969, are closely parallel.

For the complete background papers and final position paper, *see* Coriden, J., ed., *The Once & Future Church: A Communion of Freedom*, New York, NY, Alba, 1971.

For a review of this work, *see* Granfield, P. *The Jurist*, 32 (1972) 301-302.

Co-responsibility in the Church.

The sixth symposium was co-sponsored by the CLSA and Fordham University and was held in April, 1970, at Cathedral College, New York. Thirty-eight international scholars, including historians, theologians, sociologists, and canonists, focused on the theme of co-responsibility.

For the complete background papers and the final statement of consensus, *see The Jurist*, 31 (1971) 1-293; *or* Coriden, J., ed., *Who Decides for the Church?* Hartford, CT, CLSA, 1971.

The Future Discipline of Priestly Celibacy.

The seventh symposium sponsored by the CLSA was held in August, 1971, at Douglaston, New York.

This symposium assessed the desires of priests to have the option of marriage and the motives for such a choice. The dimensions of the problem in the United States of voluntary resignation of priests and the problem of priestly celibacy are examined and some historical background is provided. As a conclusion some practical recommendations are offered.

For a report on this symposium, *see The Jurist*, 32 (1972) 273-289. (*Also*, *Origins*, v. 1, 249-254 & 263-267.)

Complete background papers were not published as a unit. For most of the papers, *see* Bassett, W., & Huizing, P., *Celibacy in the Church. See also* Lynch, J., "Marriage and Celibacy of the Clergy, the Discipline of the Western Church: An Historico-Canonical Synopsis"; and, O'Meara, T., "Optional Ministerial Celibacy: Its Effect on Religious Life."

Women and Church Law

The eighth symposium sponsored by the CLSA was held in October,

1976, at Rosemont College, Rosemont, PA.

Twenty-four men and women—theologians, canonists and scholars from other fields—met to discern a number of areas that must be taken into consideration if the equality of all the baptized is to be recognized and respected. Reviewing several basic themes such as Christian anthropology, historical-theological considerations and ministry in the Church, the participants discussed discrimination in both Church law and in the attitudes of Church people. Recommendations are then offered to the CLSA, the Church at large, the clergy, and all Catholic men and women.

For a consensus statement issued at the conclusion of the symposium, see '76 *Proceedings*, 183-193; *or The Jurist*, 37 (1977) 313-324.

For the complete background papers, *see* Coriden, J., ed., *Sexism and Church Law: Equal Rights and Affirmative Action*, New York, NY, Paulist, 1977.

For a review of this work, *see*McDermott, R., *The Jurist*, 40 (1980) 218-221.

CLSA Think Tank, *An Agenda for the Future.* (*See Origins*, v. 4, 129-134, and '74 *Proceedings*, 122-129.)

In May, 1974, at Cathedral College, Douglaston, NY, two dozen men and women—bishops, theologians, canonists, religious laity, Blacks, Spanish-Americans—met to discuss the needs of the Church, to identify areas of research and study, and to assist in prioritizing an agenda for the next ten years for the CLSA. A consensus of the participants in this unique assembly led to a three-fold goal in the areas of (a) the Church as an ordered *communio*, (b) the Church in dialogue with secular society, and (c) the expanding concept of ministry within the Church. The realization of these goals was seen to involve research, development, legal reform, technical assistance, and massive education. Immediately after this meeting the Board of Governors of the CLSA acted to implement those projects and policies which were appropriate to the Society. *See* CLSA, Permanent Seminar, and Alesandro, J., "Colloquium: Notre Dame University, May 4-7, 1975."

CLSA Workshop on *Community Life and Experimentation.*

This workshop was sponsored by the CLSA and held in August, 1968, at St. Mary's College, Notre Dame, Indiana. The workshop presented a study of religious community life from the viewpoint of many different disciplines and provided a forum for discussion of some significant experiments being conducted in religious communities. For the material presented in the conferences, *see* O'Rourke, K., *Renewal Through Community and Experimentation*, Hartford, CT, CLSA, 1968.

Code of Professional Responsibility, *The Jurist*, 39 (1979) 487-493. (*Also*, '79 *Proceedings*.)
    This code was adopted by the CLSA at its 1979 annual convention. It spells out the ideals and duties of the canonist and the enforcement of the code itself.

Code, Proposed New, *see*

CLSA, "A Statement Concerning the Revision of the Code of Canon Law."

CLSA Publications, '80 *Proceedings*.

Critique of the Proposed Schemata, Hartford, CT, CLSA, (no date given).

Green, T., "Educating for the New Law—A Proposal for a Commentary."

Green, T., "Procedural Law: Reflections on the Proposed Schema."

Green, T., et al., "Reflections on Other Parts of the Proposed Draft *De Sacramentis*."

Green, T., "Reflections on the People of God Schema."

Green, T., et al., "Report of the Special Committee of the Task Force of the Canon Law Society of America on the Proposed Schema *De Delictis et Poenis*."

Green, T., et al., "Report of a Special Committee of the Task Force of the Canon Law Society of America on the marriage Canons of the Proposed Schema *Documenti Pontificii quo Disciplina Canonica de Sacramentis Recognoscitur*."

Green, T., "Sacramental Law: Reflections on the Proposed Schema."

Harman, F., "Statement by the C.L.S.A. on the Revision of the Code and a Commentary."

LaDue, W., et al., "A General Analysis of the Proposed Schema on the *Lex Fundamentalis*."

Morrisey, F., "The Current Status of Procedural Law."

Morrisey, F., "Proposed Legislation on Defective Matrimonial Consent."

O'Rourke, K., "The New Law for Religious: Principles, Content and Evaluation."

Provost, J., "Revision of Book V of the Code of Canon Law. Discussion of Tentative Draft."

Coleman, John, "The Mission of the Church and Action on Behalf of Justice," *The Jurist,* 39 (1979) 119-151.

The author turns to the Church's social teaching and related theological developments in order to focus the mission concerns of the Church in terms raised by Guttierez's claim that there are two paramount pastoral problems of our age. These are the self-proclaimed historical autonomy of the present generation in the developed world and the other two-thirds of humanity who are hungry, ill-housed, and without hope for political and material improvement of their lives. *See* CLSA Permanent Seminar.

Collegiality, *see*

Bourke, M., "Collegial Decision Making in the New Testament."

CLSA Symposia, *Unity and Subsidiarity in the Church: Rome and the Conference of Bishops.*

Greeley, A.,"A Social Organizational View of the Catholic Church."

Komonchak, J., "A New Law for the People of God: Some Theological Reflections."

McBrien, R., "A Preliminary Ecclesiological Statement."

Padovano, A., "A Theology of Church Government."

Tierney, B., "Roots of Western Constitutionalism."

Collins, Patrick W., "Ministry to Separated, Divorced and Remarried Persons," *The Living Light,* 13 (1976) 545-546.

The chairperson of the CLSA Committee on Continuing Education introduces a special issue for religious educators. *See* CLSA, Committee on Continuing Education.

Commitment, Permanent, *see*

Jegen, C., "Theological Consideration on the Problematic of Permanent Commitment."

Westley, R., "The Problematic of Permanent Commitment."

Common Good, *see* Dupré, L. & C., "The Indissolubility of Christian Marriage and the Common Good."

Common Law, *see* Orsy, L., "The Dynamic Spirit of Common Law and the Renewal of Canon Law."

Common Law, *see* Orsy, L., "The Dynamic Spirit of Common Law and the Renewal of Canon Law."

Common Sources of Nullity, *see* Wrenn, L.

Communio, *see*

    CLSA Symposia, *Unity and Subsidiarity in the Church: Rome and the Conference of Bishops.*

    Kress, R., "The Church as *Communio*: Trinity and Incarnation as the Foundation of Ecclesiology."

    Lynch, J., "The Limits of *Communio* in the Pre-Constantinian Church."

    Provost, J., "Structuring the Church as a *Communio*."

    Prusak, B., "Hospitality Extended or Denied: *Koinōnia* Incarnate from Jesus to Augustine."

    van der Poel, C., "Marriage and Family as Expressions of *Communio* in the Church."

Communion, First, *see* Buckley, F., "The Right to the Sacraments of Initiation."

Community, *see*

    Benson, R., "Election by Community and Chapter: Reflection on Co-responsibility in the Historical Church."

    Boyle, P., ed., *Selected Passages from Religious Constitutions Dealing with the Evangelical Counsels and Community Life.*

    CLSA Workshop on *Community Life and Experimentation.*

    Fahey, M., "Ecclesial Community as Communion."

    Murray, J.C., "Freedom, Authority, Community."

    Padovano, A., "A Theology of Church Government."

    Swift, T., "The Human Dimension of Authority and Obedience in a Faith Community."

Conciliar Legislation, Baltimore, *see* Burns, D., et al., "Committee Report on Legislation of Councils of Baltimore.

Conciliarism, *see* McNeill, J., "The Relevance of Conciliarism."

Conciliation, *see* Due Process.

Confidentiality, *see*

Dillon, E., "*De Processibus:* An Analysis of Some Key Provisions."

Geary, P., "Civil Discovery and Confidentiality of Church Documents."

Confirmation, *see*

Buckley, F., "The Right to the Sacraments of Initiation."

Green, T. et al., "Reflection on Other Parts of the Proposed Draft *De Sacramentis.*"

Congregation for Catholic Education, Sacred, *see* Golden, P. & Green, T., "Teaching Canon Law Today."

Congregation for the Doctrine of the Faith, Sacred, *see* Finnegan, J., "Spiritual Direction for the Catholic Divorced and Remarried."

Conroy, Donald B., "The Statistics and Crisis of Divorce," *The Living Light*, 13 (1976) 547-552.

In light of current statistics on divorce, the situation of divorced and remarried persons demands a specialized ministry from the Church. Conroy suggests certain elements needed for the effectiveness of such ministry. *See* CLSA, Committee on Continuing Education.

"Canonical Challenges in the Pastoral Ministry of Families," '78 *Proceedings*, 7-12.

The author offers a commentary on the 1978 NCCB "Plan of Pastoral Action for Family Ministry," addressing the notion of "total family ministry"; viz., ministry to the engaged, to married couples, to mixed marriages, and to separated and divorced Catholics.

Conscience, *see* Curran, C., "Law and Conscience in the Christian Context."

Consent, *see* Marriage Consent.

Constance, Council of, *see* Tierney, B., "Roots of Western Constitutionalism."

Constantelos, Demetrios, "Marriage and Celibacy of the Clergy in the Orthodox Church," *Celibacy in the Church*, 30-38.

The history of Orthodox practice is reviewed in light of the theological arguments for various positions. Current issues of remarriage by widowed clergy, and restriction of the episcopate to celibates, are also outlined. *See* CLSA Symposia, *The Future Discipline of Priestly Celibacy.*

Constitutionalism, *see*

CLSA Symposia, *A Constitution for the Church.*

Hess, H., "Authority: Its Source, Nature and Purpose in the Church."

Tierney, B., "Roots of Western Constitutionalism."

Contraception, *see* Crowley, P. & P., "The Meaning of Conjugal Love."

Conveyance, (formerly termed "alienation") *see*

Bevilacqua, A., "Problem Areas in Chancery Practice."

Morrisey, F., "The Conveyance of Ecclesiastical Goods."

Co-responsibility, *see*

Benson, R., "Election by Community and Chapter: Reflection of Co-responsibility in the Historical Church."

CLSA Symposia, *Co-responsibility in the Church.*

Curran, C., "Responsibility in Moral Theology: Centrality, Foundations, and Implications for Ecclesiology."

Gumbleton, T., "The Diocesan Synod of Detroit: Renewal in Process."

Gumbleton, T., "Due Process in the Church."

Heintschel, D., "Participative Leadership and Shared Responsibility in the Church."

Lynch, J., "Co-responsibility in the First Five Centuries: Presbyteral Colleges and the Election of Bishops."

Morrissey, M., "Issues in Chancery Practice."

Coriden, James, ed., *We the People of God . . . A Study of Constitutional Government for the Church,* Huntington, IN, Our Sunday Visitor Press, 1968. *See* CLSA Symposia, *A Constitution for the Church*

For a review of this work, *see* Orsy, L., *The Jurist,* 29 (1969) 210-215.

ed., *The Case for Freedom: Human Rights in the Church,* Washington, D.C., Corpus, 1969. *See* CLSA Symposia, *Rights in the Church.*

For a review of this work, *see* Banks, R., *The Jurist,* 30 (1970) 230-241.

ed., *The Once & Future Church: A Communion of Freedom,* New York, NY, Alba, 1971. *See* CLSA Symposia, *Unity and Subsidiarity in the Church.*

For a review of this work, *see* Granfield, P., *The Jurist,* 32 (1972) 301-302.

ed., *Who Decides for the Church?* Hartford, CT, CLSA, 1971. *See* CLSA Symposia, *Co-responsibility in the Church.*

This work is published as both a separate book and in *The Jurist*, 31 (1971) 1-293.

"Ministry," *The Pastoral Guide to Canon Law*, 305-315.

The meaning of ministry, its goals and responsibilities, as well as who may do ministry in the Church are explained in question and answer format. *See* CLSA Committee on Continuing Education.

ed., *Sexism and Church Law: Equal Rights and Affirmative Action*, New York, NY, Paulist, 1977. *See* CLSA Symposia, *Women and Church Law.*

For a review of this work, *see* McDermott, R., *The Jurist*, 40 (1980) 218-221.

& Mangan, Martin, "Team Ministry," '72 *Proceedings*, 70-75.

This is a CLSA seminar which outlines Team Ministry's background, canonical aspects, and resources in addition to the practical aspects from the experience of Team Ministry at St. Mary's Parish, Taylorville, Illinois.

Crossan, Dominic, "Divorce and Remarriage in the New Testament," *The Bond of Marriage*, 1-33.

The strong stand of Jesus against divorce and the exceptions made by the early Christian community are examined in themselves and with application to the modern setting. *See* CLSA Symposia, *The Bond of Marriage.*

Crosson, Frederick J., "Liberty and Authority in the Church," *Law for Liberty*, 147-155.

Crosson explores the political and family dimensions of Church law, pointing to how much canon law draws on both approaches. *See* CLSA Symposia, *The Role of Law in the Church.*

Crowley, Pat & Patty, "The Meaning of Conjugal Love," '73 *Proceedings*, 8-12.

Christian Family Movement President Couple discuss marriage, birth control, and love.

Cuenin, Walter, "The Marriage of Baptized Non-Believers: Questions of Faith, Sacrament and Law," '78 *Proceedings*, 38-48. (*Also, Origins*, v. 8, 321-328.)

The author argues that faith is necessary for a sacramental marriage and this should be incorporated into the proposed new Code. When faith is totally absent the Church should refuse the sacrament but recognize the marriages of baptized non-believers as valid and human. Cuenin offers some general principles and practical directions for addressing this problem.

Cuneo, J. James, "The Power of jurisdiction: Empowerment for Church Functioning and Mission Distinct from the Power of Orders," *The Jurist*, 39 (1979) 183-219.

Cuneo draws on external sources and canonical research for an understanding of mission and challenges American canonists by raising stimulating possibilities for mission now and in the future. *See* CLSA Permanent Seminar.

Cunningham, Agnes, "Church People as Missionary: A Ministerial Church," *The Jurist*, 39 (1979) 152-182.

Cunningham draws on linguistic analysis and early Christian life in order to show that ministry is not a restrictive concept, but one which broadens the understanding of each Christian's relationship to the world when placed in the perspective of *missio*. *See* CLSA Permanent Seminar.

Cunningham, Richard, "Recent Rotal Decisions and Today's Marriage Theology: Nothing Has Changed—Or Has It?" '76 *Proceedings*, 24-41. (*Also*, Origins, v. 6, 300-304.)

Cunningham presents a study of fifty Rotal decisions in the areas of consent, capacity, conjugal love and consortium, and applies his findings to the theology of marriage today.

Curran, Charles E., "Law and Conscience in the Christian Context," *Law for Liberty*, 156-171.

After exploring the concept of positive law in the Church, Curran develops the relationship between law and sin and explores the role of *Epikeia* in Church life. *See* CLSA Symposia, *The Role of Law in the Church.*

"Responsibility in Moral Theology: Centrality, Foundations, and Implications for Ecclesiology," *The Jurist*, 31 (1971) 113-142.

The author discusses the theological foundation of co-responsiblity. He offers reasons why responsibility has become a normative model and theme in today's Christian ethics and the drastic changes that will affect ecclesiology on the level of institution and structure if it is to be adopted by the Church. Curran understands co-responsibility in the Church

as primarily involving the covenant commitment of the individual
believer to the Lord and to his fellow believers in the ecclesial community and all that flows from this commitment. See CLSA Symposia,
Co-Responsibility in the Church.

"Divorce—From the Perspective of Moral Theology," '74 *Proceedings*,
1-24. (*Also* an excerpt in *Origins*, v. 4, 329-335.)

This study identifies the principal signs of the times and evaluates them
in the light of contemporary moral theology. It discusses the methodo-
logical use of the Scriptures in moral theology, the influence of the shift
to historical consciousness, the effect of a more personalist approach,
and the implications of eschatological considerations. Curran's conclusion is that the Roman Catholic Church should change its teaching on
divorce.

-D-

Deacon, *see*

Nardoni, E., "Ministries in the New Testament."

Hedderman, J., "The Permanent Diaconate: Its Development and Its
Canonical Implications."

Decisions, see Wrenn, L.

De Episcoporum Muneribus, *see* Ryan, R., "The Dispensing Authority of
the Residential Bishop."

Detroit, Archdiocese of, *see*

Brunett, A., "The Diocesan Synod of Detroit: The Theology Underlying
the Synod Document."

Gumbleton, T., "The Diocesan Synod of Detroit: Renewal in Process."

Detroit Conference, *see* Finnegan, J., "The Detroit Conference—'A Call to
Action'—As a Model of Church Governance."

Dillon, Edward, ed., *Matrimonial Jurisprudence, United States 1972*, Toledo,
OH, CLSA, 1974.

"*De processibus*: An Analysis of Some Key Provisions," '80 *Proceedings*,
161-170.

Issues of the number of judges on a case, competence of the tribunal,
confidentiality, and appeal are reviewed in the light of current American

practice. A special survey of personnel and budget developments over the last several years in American tribunals is included, along with recommendations from various round-table discussions conducted during the seminar.

Dillon, Richard, "Theory and Norms of the Governing Ministry Derived from the Gospel of St. Matthew," '72 *Proceedings*, 34-53.

This is an examination of Matthew and how the Church which accepted his book understood itself. Matthew offers no structure nor explicit theory of Church government but Dillon suggests that in Matthew there is at least a basis of an ideology of leadership in the Church. By inference, the author analyzes three terms of the Lord's mandate: viz., make disciples, teach, observe what has been commanded.

Diocesan Structures, *see*

Brunett, A., "The Diocesan Synod of Detroit."

Gumbleton, T., " The Diocesan Synod in Detroit: Renewal in Process."

Mallett, J., "Diocesan Structure and Governance."

Discussion on the Motu Proprio Ecclesiae Sanctae, see Boyle, P., ed.

Disobedience, Ecclesial, *see* Banks, R., "Ecclesial Disobedience."

Disparity of Cult, *see* Bevilacqua, A., "Problem Areas in Chancery Practice."

Dispensations, ibid.

Dispensed Priests, *see*

CLSA, "Dispensed Priests in Ecclesial Ministry: A Canonical Reflection."

See also Laicization of Priests.

Dispensing Authority, *see* Ryan, R., "The Dispensing Authority of the Residential Bishop."

Divorce, *see*

Bernardin, J., "Keynote Address."

CLSA, Committee on Alternatives to Tribunal Procedures, "Statement."

CLSA, Committee on Continuing Education.

CLSA Publications, *Audio-Visual Learning on Marriage, Divorce, Tribunal Practice.*

Conroy, D., "Canonical Challenges in the Pastoral Ministry of Families."

Crosson, D., "Divorce and Remarriage in the New Testament."

Curran, C., "Divorce—From the Perspective of Moral Theology."

Finnegan, J., "Spiritual Direction for the Catholic Divorced and Remarried."

Hern, K., "A Positive Approach from Civil Law."

MacRae, G., "New Testament Perspectives on Marriage and Divorce."

Noonan, J. "Novel 22."

Wrenn, L., *Divorce and Remarriage in the Catholic Church.*

See also, Children of Divorce.

Document of Liberty, *see*

Carney, R., "New Applications of Canon 1127."

Orsy, L., "An Evaluation of 'New Applications of Canon 1127.' "

Dogma, Christian, *see* Meyendorff, J., "Historical Relativism and Authority in Christian Dogma."

Dogma and Law, *see* Pelikan, J., "Law and Dogma: Some Historical Interrelations."

Dolciamore, John, ed., *Matrimonial Jurisprudence, United States, 1968-1971*, Hartford CT, CLSA, 1973.

"Interpersonal Relationships and Their Effect on the Validity of Marriages," '73 *Proceedings*, 84-100.

The author presents a seminar on the effect of psychological problems on the validity of marriage. Dolciamore offers a survey of the methods by which these grounds are handled in various tribunals and the on-going development of the grounds.

A review of L. Wrenn's *Divorce and Remarriage in the Catholic Church*, *The Jurist*, 34 (1974) 202-208.

Douglaston, *see* CLSA Think Tank.

Doyle, Thomas P., ed., *Marriage Studies I*, Toledo, OH, CLSA, 1980. *See* CLSA Committee on Marriage Research.

"The Canonical Foundations for Pre-Marriage Preparation Guidelines," *Marriage Studies I*, 65-77.

The basis for marriage preparation guidelines are evaluated in terms of the responsibility of the pastor to determine freedom to marry, restrictions on the marriages of minors, and provisions in the law relative to delay and prohibition of marriage.

"Select Bibliography on the Sacrament of Marriage," *Marriage Studies I*, 78-101.

A wide-ranging bibliography on a chronological basis, including primary and secondary sources.

& Licari, Ronald, " 'Everything You Ever Wanted to Know About the Competent Forum But Were Afraid to Ask,' " *Marriage Studies I*, 102-143.

The restriction on competence of American tribunals under the American Procedural Norms is discussed in light of the declaration from the Apostolic Signatura, April 12, 1978. Appendices are given with the declaration of the Signatura and a commentary by Zenon Grocholewski.

Dozier, Carroll, "Rights of People in the Church: A Pastor Speaks," '79 *Proceedings*, 12-18.

The author discusses the tension between the role of law and the person who lives within and under that role. Dozier states that the Church Law must reach out concretely to contemporary man as a forum for fostering basic human rights and, therefore, Christian rights.

Dreher, John, "New Wineskins for New Wine. The Need for Pastoral Planning and Leadership Development for a Church in Transition," '76 *Proceedings*, 99-106.

The author, a pastoral planner, drawing on the experiences of the Diocese of Providence, looks at the situation of the Church today and the need for new leadership systems, styles, tools and skills. Dreher offers a consideration of how these needs relate to canonists.

Druckman, Joan M., "Interaction Styles and Background Characteristics of Pre-Marital Couples," *Marrige Studies* I, 41-64.

Based on a sampling of 123 pre-marital couples, interaction styles and background are analyzed. Appendices and tables are provided.

Due Process, CLSA, "*Nihil Obstat* for Due Process," *The Jurist*, 32 (1972) 291-292.

The CLSA prepared a plan for due process which was approved by the NCCB in November, 1969 and received a *nihil obstat* from Pope Paul VI in October, 1971. The material is published in booklet form and is entitled *On Due Process*. There are two publishers, Hartford, CT, CLSA, 1970; and Washington, D.C., USCC Publications Office, 1970, *Revised Edition*, 1972.

See also Gumbleton, T., "Due Process in the Church."

Kennedy, R., "Address on Due Process to the National Conference of Catholic Bishops."

Kennedy, R., ed., *Due Process: Blueprint for Procedural Fairness in the Church.*

Kennedy, R., et al., "Report of the *Ad Hoc* Committee on Due Process to the Canon Law Society of America."

Kennedy, R., ed., *Report of the Committee on Due Process.*

Mahoney, R., "Due Process Within the National Conference of Catholic Bishops."

Molloy, T., "The Theological Foundation of Ecclesiastical Due Process."

Dunning, James B., "Two Fly Into the Lovebird's Nest, Or Catechesis for Building the Covenant," *The Living Light*, 13 (1976) 601-611.

Values and decision-making are discussed in view of their effect on marriage. Dunning argues for the role of catechists in such long-range preparation for married life. *See* CLSA, Committee on Continuing Education.

Dupré, Louis and Constance, "The Indissolubility of Christian Marriage and the Common Good," *The Bond of Marriage*, 181-199.

The traditional opposition of the Church to divorce is set in the context of traditional Catholic social teaching about the common good. The question is then raised, what sort of marital stability does the balance of common good between society as a whole and the rights of its individuals require today. Several aspects of the question are explored, but the bottom line is the significance of fidelity as an indispensible element in marital relationship. *See* CLSA Symposia, *The Bond of Marriage.*

Dvornik, Francis, "Origin of Episcopal Synods," *The Once & Future Church*, 25-56.

The "permanent synod" in the Eastern church is explored in its historical roots and practice, as well as the practice in the Diocese of Rome. *See* CLSA Symposia, *Unity and Subsidiarity in the Church.*

-E-

Eastern Rites, *see*

Logar, W., "Liberty and Justice for All: An Ecclesial Interpretation."

Wojnar, M., "Participation of the Clergy and Laity in the Election of Bishops According to the Discipline of the Oriental Catholic Churches."

See also Oriental Church.

Ecclesiae Sanctae, *see* Boyle, P. ed., *Discussions on the Motu Proprio Ecclesiae Sanctae.*

Ecclesiastical Goods, *see* Morrisey, F., "The Conveyance of Ecclesiastical Goods."

Ecclesiology, *see*

Curran, C., "Responsibility in Moral Theology: Centrality, Foundations, and Implications for Ecclesiology."

Goedert, R., "Selection of Bishops. A Canonical and Pastoral Critique of the New Norms."

Kennedy, R., "The Early Republic's Challenge to Catholic Church Governance: Bicentennial Reflections of an American Canonist."

Kress, R., "The Church as *Communio*: Trinity and Incarnation as the Foundation of Ecclesiology."

McNally, R., "The Tridentine Church: A Study in Ecclesiology."

Ecumenical Marriages, *see*

Bevilacqua, A., "Problem Areas in Chancery Practice."

Knox, L., "Marriage and Ministry: Some Ecumenical Reflections."

Lynch, J., "Ecumenical Marriages."

Wynn, J., "Prevailing and Countervailing Trends in the Non-Catholic Churches."

Ecumenism, *see*

Bowen, H., "Ecumenism and the Local Community."

Boyle, P., "The Renewal of Canon Law and the Resolutions of the Canon Law Society of America, 1965."

Bridston, K., "The Polity and Politics of Church Unity."

Green, T., et al., "Reflections on Other Parts of the Proposed Draft *De Sacramentis.*"

Green, T., "Reflections on the People of God Schema."

Law, B., "Ecumenism in U.S.A.—Problems and Prospects."

Lynch, J., "Ecumenical Guidelines."

Moreau, J., "Choosing Bishops in the Anglican Communion."

Ozment, S., "Marriage and the Ministry in the Protestant Churches."

Election, *see*

Benson, R., "Election by Community and Chapter: Reflections on Co-responsibility in the Historical Church."

Lynch, J., "Co-responsibility in the First Five Centuries: Presbyteral Colleges and the Election of Bishops."

Elizondo, Virgil, "The Spanish Speaking and the Law," '75 *Proceedings,* 101-105.

The rapid increase of Spanish speaking persons in the United States is addressed by the author in the light of two major problems that demand immediate action; viz., the efforts of the United Farm Workers to insure free elections, and the massive deportation of so called "illegals." While working to correct economic injustices, Elizondo points out that the life-giving mission of the Spirit demands that we not only respect the ethnos of other peoples but also help to promote it and to grow with it.

Ellis, John T., "Those Called to Lead—Then and Now," '72 *Proceedings,* 4-33. (*Also, Origins,* v. 2, 317-331.)

With an historian's vision, Ellis raises the questions, what should a bishop do once he is selected and how can he offer inspiration and leadership in a period of change and ferment that is revolutionary? The author considers an American view and a world view of Catholicism, examining the past and the present and offering the opinions of his respected lay friends.

Epikeia, see Curran, C., "Law and Conscience in the Christian Context."

Episcopal Conferences, *see*

Heston, E., "Present Organizational Design and Structure of the Roman Catholic Church."

Huizing, P., "The Structure of Episcopal Conferences."

-F-

Fahey, Michael, "Ecclesial Community as Communion," *The Jurist*, 36 (1976) 4-23.

Together with a theological overview, the author offers an analysis of the scriptural and patristic terms and some Christian insights relative to *communio. See* CLSA Permanent Seminar.

Faith, *see*

Cuenin, W., "The Marriage of Baptized Non-Believers: Questions of Faith, Sacrament and Law."

O'Rourke, J., "The Faith Required for the Privilege of the Faith Dispensation."

Faith, Favor of the, *see*

Carney, R., "New Applications of Canon 1127."

O'Rourke, J., "The Faith Required for the Privilege of the Faith Dispensation."

Orsy, L., "An Evaluation of 'New Applications of Canon 1127.' "

Faith, Good, *see* Carey, R., "The Good Faith Solution."

Family, *see*

Conroy, D., "Canonical Challenges in the Pastoral Ministry of Families."

Greeley, A., "Church Marriage Procedures and the Contemporary Family."

McDaniel, H., "A Social Agency Looks at the Family."

Sussman, M., "The Family in the 1960's: Facts, Fictions, Problems, Prospects and Institutional Linkages."

van der Poel, C., "Marriage and Family as Expressions of *Communio* in the Church."

Farley, Leo & Reick, Warren, "Toward 'An Immediate Internal Forum Solution' for Deserving Couples in Canonically Insoluble Marriage Cases," *The Jurist*, 30 (1970) 45-74.

This is a part of the report of the *ad hoc* Committee appointed by the CLSA to investigate immediate internal forum solutions for deserving persons involved in canonically insoluble marriage cases. For the entire work, *see* Orsy, L., et al., "Intolerable Marriage Situations: Conflict between External and Internal Forum," *The Jurist*, 30 (1970) 1-74.

Farrell, William P., "A Parish Plan for Ministry to Divorced Catholics," *The Living Light,* 13 (1976) 582-587.

A director of religious education provides an outline and suggested materials for a parish session on behalf of divorced Catholics. *See* CLSA, Committee on Continuing Education.

Fellhauer, David E., *see* Morrisey, F., Fellhauer, D., & Alesandro, J., "Marriage Legislation in the New Code."

Fidelity, *see*

Bourke, V., "Marital Fidelity and Philosophy."

Brown, R., "Non-inclusion: A Form of Simulation."

Dupré, L. & C., "The Indissolubility of Christian Marriage and the Common Good."

Finnegan, John, "When is a Marriage Indissoluble? Reflections on a Contemporary Understanding of a Ratified and Consummated Marriage?" *The Jurist,* 28 (1968) 309-329.

This paper was presented at the CLSA's Eastern Regional Meeting at Atlantic City, N.J. in 1968. The author expresses his belief that the correct question that must be asked is, "When is a marriage sacramental and Christian?" After setting down guidelines, he offers an historical search and a contemporary understanding of the "when" in terms of a study of the meaning of the words *"ratum et consummatum."* Finnegan concludes with a look to the future and the need for the Church to shift her pastoral care and solicitude from the "when" to the "how" of Christian marriage.

"The Capacity to Marry," *The Jurist,* 29 (1969) 141-156.

This paper was presented at the Annual Convention of the CLSA at Boston, Massachusetts in 1968. The author offers a number of proposals in regard to the psychological capacity necessary to enter marriage in our age and culture, and the consequent need for a greater emphasis on counseling. He outlines a plan for adapting the stages of psychological change that result from counseling to use as a counseling instrument for the bringing about of moral change. Finnegan concludes with practical suggestions as to how this could be effected.

"The Present Canonical Practice in the Catholic Church," in Bassett, W., ed., *The Choosing of Bishops,* 85-102.

Within the context of canonical tradition and the present Code of canon law, the existing norms from 1916 which applied in the United States for selecting bishops are detailed and critiqued with a view to developments in the Second Vatican Council. *See* CLSA, Committee on the Selection of Bishops.

"Spiritual Direction for the Catholic Divorced and Remarried," '73 *Proceedings*, 70-83.

The author discusses the peculiar problem of the Catholic who is divorced, and offers a tentative program of pastoral care with suggestions for the priest as spiritual director and discerner. Finnegan concludes with his own interpretation of the 1973 Letter of the Sacred Congregation for the Doctrine of the Faith regarding those "living in an irregular union."

"Marriage/Pastoral Care," *Origins*, v. 5, 150-157.

As President of the CLSA, the author testifies before the U.S. Bishops' Committee for the Bicentennial. He states that a new theology of marriage is emerging but the Church's pastoral practice has lagged behind, offering inadequate care at every phase of marital life, including marriage preparation, family life and help for divorced Catholics. Finnegan calls upon the bishops to develop pastoral care and marriage support programs.

"An Agenda for Dialogue Between Catholic Feminists and Church Authorities," *Sexism and Church Law*, 136-149.

Finnegan argues for gradualism in the dialogue, and identifies several canonical, liturgical and practical areas where the dialogue can be carried on. *See* CLSA Symposia, *Women and Church Law*.

"Marriage Law," *The Pastoral Guide to Canon Law*, 281-304.

Basic issues of canon law on marriage, including the meaning of marriage, what it takes to be married, and the role of church tribunals, are explained in question and answer form. *See* CLSA Committee on Continuing Education.

"The Detroit Conference—'A Call to Action'—As a Model of Church Governance," '77 *Proceedings*, 10-18.

This is an examination of the NCCB sponsored 1976 Detroit Conference, its strengths and its weaknesses and its value as a model form for governance in the Church.

Fiscal Administration, *see* Bennett, A., "The Practical Effects on the Fiscal Administration of Church Finances of the Provisions of Book Five."

Foley, Nadine, "Woman in Vatican Documents 1960 to the Present," *Sexism and Church Law*, 82-108.

A careful evaluation of Vatican documents reveals a distinct ontology about the nature of women. An alternative ontology is suggested, with possible changes in conclusions reached in the documents. *See* CLSA Symposia, *Women and Church Law.*

Fontinell, Eugene, "Authority and Freedom in the Christian Community, Expressed in the Structures of the Institution," *We, The People of God . . . ,* 159-172.

A series of propositions are submitted to explore the implications of reform for Church structures, the role of institutions in reform, and how authority and freedom are affected by these in the structural institution of the Christian community. *See* CLSA Symposia, *A Constitution for the Church.*

Francis, Joseph, "The Canonists—Advocate," '78 *Proceedings,* 1-6.

The author asks canonists to empower persons by becoming advocates for justice in the local Church. Give witness, Francis says, to Jesus' presence among us by involvement in advocacy for justice.

Freedom, *see*

Bassett, W., "Subsidiarity, Order and Freedom in the Church."

CLSA Symposia, *Rights in the Church.*

CLSA Symposia, *Unity and Subsidiarity in the Church: Rome and the Conference of Bishops.*

Fontinell, E., "Authority and Freedom in the Christian Community, Expressed in the Structures of the Institution."

Meyer, C., "Christian Freedom."

Murray, J.C., "Freedom, Authority, Community."

O'Dea, T., "Authority and Freedom in the Church: Tension, Balance and Contradiction: An Historico-Sociological View."

See also Liberty.

-G-

Galante, Joseph, *see* O'Connor, D. et al., "Current Issues in Religious Law."

Gaudium et Spes, see Hehir, J.B., "The Church in Mission: Canonical Implications."

Geary, Patrick, "Civil Discovery and Confidentiality of Church Documents," '77 *Proceedings*, 82-86.

The author examines the Federal Rules of Discovery and the priest/penitent privilege of immunity statute in relationship to Tribunal documents, especially the vulnerability of those documents which contain the testimony of third parties.

Gill, James J., "Psychological Impact of the Change to Optional Celibacy," *Celibacy in the Church*, 95-108.

Psychologist Gill explores emotional, social and cultural questions which a change to optional celibacy would raise in the Church community. He suggests twelve principles which might help the Church community through such a transition. *See* CLSA Symposia, *The Future Discipline of Priestly Celibacy.*

Goedert, Raymond, "Selection of Bishops. A Canonical and Pastoral Critique of the New Norms," '72 *Proceedings*, 54-61.

On March 25, 1972, the Holy See issued the decree, "The Selection of Candidates for the Episcopacy in the Latin Church." Under the headings of ecclesiology, subsidiarity, consultation and methodology, the author examines this document.

Gokey, Francis, "The Relationship of Religious to the Local Church," '73 *Proceedings*, 106-111.

From his experience with the Conference of Major Superiors of Men, the author speaks of the place of religious in the local Church. Gokey offers a theological basis for a collaboration of religious with the local Church.

Golden, Paul, "Teaching Canon Law," '73 *Proceedings*, 101-105.

The author presents a seminar on the necessity of studying Canon Law, the curriculum today, the art of teaching Canon Law and continuing education programs.

& Green, Thomas, "Teaching Canon Law Today," '76 *Proceedings*, 42-51.

This is a brief paper on how teachers evaluate their own programs. Golden then reflects on the "Letter of the Sacred Congregation for Catholic Education on the Teaching of Canon Law," (April 2, 1975). A copy of the letter is included.

& Hill, Richard, "Report on Survey of Teachers of Canon Law," '78 *Proceedings*, 117-124.

This survey aims at identifying the teacher of Canon Law, the students of Canon Law, and the curriculum in Canon Law in seminaries and theological schools in the United States.

Good Faith Solution, *see* Carey, R., "The Good Faith Solution."

Gorman, John, "Young Priests in Transition," '69 *Proceedings*, 96-101.
The author describes some of the shifts in emphasis that are characteristic of young priests as they enter the ministry today. Areas of cultural changes, theology, commitment, type of ministry, priority differences, leadership, law and other questions are discussed as points of difference between older and younger priests that cause tensions. Gorman expresses the hope that this will be a creative tension in the ministry of the seventies.

Gospel, *see*
Ahern, B., "Law and the Gospel."
See also Mathew, St.; New Testament; Scripture and Canon Law.

Governance, Church, *see* Church Governance.

Governance, Religious, *see* Institutes of Life.

Governing Ministry, *see* Dillon, R., "Theory and Norms of the Governing Ministry Derived from the Gospel of St. Matthew."

Graham, George, "Personality Disorders and Their Effect on the Validity of Marriage," '76 *Proceedings*, 138-149. (*Also, Origins*, v. 6, 304-308.)
This is a seminar discussion of three marriage cases involving those disorders called the hysterical personality, the inadequate personality and the anti-social personality. The author examines the effects of these disorders on the validity of marriage.

Granfield, Patrick, A review of J. Coriden's *The Once & Future Church: A Communion of Freedom, The Jurist,* 32 (1972) 301-302.

Greeley, Andrew, "A Social Organizational View of the Catholic Church," *We, the People of God . . . ,* 81-89.
Greeley analyzes various aspects of the operations of the Catholic Church in the United States from the point of view of social organizations, and finds a number of aspects which need further reform. *See* CLSA Symposia, *A Constitution for the Church.*

"Leadership and Friendship: A Sociologist's Viewpoint," *The Jurist*, 31 (1971) 266-279.

> After discussing an article by John Scharr, entitled "Reflections on Authority," Greeley offers his own conceptions of leadership. He states that leadership is to be at once paternal and fraternal and to involve a style that is symbolic, ideological, interpersonal, and organizational. *See* CLSA Symposia, *Co-responsibility in the Church.*

"Church Marriage Procedures and the Contemporary Family," *Divorce and Remarriage in the Catholic Church*, 105-113.

> Exploring the social interaction of marriage, the author poses several questions for possible changes in Church procedures for understanding and evaluating marriage. *See* CLSA Committee on Tribunal Decision Making.

Green, Thomas, "*Causas Matrimoniales* and the A.P.N.—A Survey," '73 *Proceedings*, 121-125.

> The author presents an overview of the responses of persons involved in Tribunal work on the impact of the possible loss of the American Procedural Norms.

et al., "Report of the Special Committee of the Task Force of the Canon Law Society of America on the Proposed Schema *De Delictis et Poenis*," '74 *Proceedings*, 130-140.

> The author says that the proposed penal law has numerous positive features but they can only be responsibly evaluated after they have been lived with for an experimental period. This critique calls for a more extended consultative process.

"Sacramental Law: Reflections on the Proposed Schema," '75 *Proceedings*, 70-83.

> This is the result of a CLSA Task Force evaluation which finds that the schema fails to adequately reflect the Second Vatican Council in some key areas; viz., that it tends to legislate answers to controverted questions and it contains legal inadequacies.

et al., "Report of a Special Committee of the Task Force of the Canon Law Society of America on the Marriage Canons of the Proposed *Schema Documenti Pontificii quo Disciplina Canonica de Sacramentis Recognoscitur*," '75 *Proceedings*, 205-217.

> This study concludes that the promulgation of this draft should be deferred indefinitely while continuing the post-conciliar pattern of legislating through *ad experimentum motu proprios*. The authors call on the bishops to initiate a broad process of consultation on sacramental law.

et al., "Reflections on Other Parts of the Proposed Draft *De Sacramentis*, '75 *Proceedings*, 194-205.

This is a critique by the CLSA Task Force on the new draft on the sacraments of Anointing of the Sick, Baptism, Penance, Orders and Eucharist. The authors offer both an ecumenical overview of the draft and an overview from the perspective of sacramental theology.

"Canonical-Pastoral Reflections on Divorce and Remarriage," *The Living Light*, 13 (1976) 560-576.

On behalf of religious educators, Green reviews the procedures for annulments, the meaning of a dissolution of bond, and pastoral processes for admission to the sacraments of penance and eucharist. *See* CLSA, Committee on Continuing Education.

"Procedural Law: Reflections on the Proposed Schema," '77 *Proceedings*, 63-81.

The author examines the critiques of the Procedural Law Schema made by the CLSA Task Force on the Revision of the Code, together with those of the Canon Law Societies of Australia, the British Isles, and Canada, and a meeting of representatives of seven episcopal conferences held at Dublin.

"Reflections on the People of God Schema," '78 *Proceedings*, 13-33.

The author examines the relationship of theology and law, the organization of the schema, the issue of basic rights and obligations, the role of women, the principle of subsidiarity, ministry, ecumenical considerations, and the need for more consultation.

"Educating for the New Law—A Proposal for a Commentary," '79 *Proceedings*, 32-36.

The author proposes a commentary on the new law to be undertaken by the CLSA and he seeks from the membership a consensus.

"Reflections on Penal Law Reform," '80 *Proceedings*, 179-187.

Key issues of penal law reform are reviewed in terms of the proposed draft for penal law in the new Code.

& Golden, Paul, "Teaching Canon Law Today," '76 *Proceedings*, 42-51.

Gregorian Reform, *see* Ryan, J.J., "Canon Law in the Gregorian Reform Epoch (c. 1050-1125): Historical Perspectives in the Present Age of Renewal."

Griffin, Bertram, "Future Challenges in the Area of Marriage Legislation," '73 *Proceedings*, 22-32.

> The author takes the position of an advocate for an unresolved but serious pastoral problem; viz., whether, in doubtful cases, considering the situation of marriage and family life in America, the legal presumption of c. 1014 can be rebutted by a judicial presumption favoring the freedom of the parties. Griffin presents the facts of his case, the pertinent jurisprudence, and the implications. He recommends that the Society develop research into the theology of marriage, and research and develop an alternative process for marriage cases that safeguards the sacred nature of the bond of marriage and the pastoral needs of the faithful.

& Burns, Dennis, "Tribunal Procedure," '72 *Proceedings*, 76-82.

Gumbleton, Thomas, "Due Process in the Church," '69 *Proceedings*, 1-9.

> The author examines the question of Due Process in the Church on the basis of some fundamental theological considerations; viz., the nature of Church, the manner in which episcopal authority is to be exercised, and co-responsibility. Gumbleton suggests some glaring failures in our law to safeguard adequately the rights of persons in the Church and he shows how a bishop who exercises his authority in a manner that guarantees every person's right to due process could be sure that his authority would be a true service to all his people in the building up of the Body of Christ.

"The Diocesan Synod in Detroit: Renewal in Process," '69 *Proceedings*, 116-121.

> The author outlines the new structure initiated to serve the needs of the Church in Detroit.

-H-

Haight, Roger, "The Established Church as Mission: The Relation of the Church to the Modern World," *The Jurist*, 39 (1979) 4-39.

> The author shows how the basic concept of mission is relational; how the primitive Church's self-understanding as mission was constitutive of the development of its formal identity and how that self-understanding is especially relevant today, even for "established" churches in the modern world. *See* CLSA Permanent Seminar.

Häring, Bernard, "Internal Forum Solutions to Insoluble Marriage Cases," *The Jurist*, 30 (1970) 21-30.

This paper is a part of the report of the *ad hoc* Committee appointed by the CLSA to investigate immediate internal forum solutions for deserving persons involved in canonically insoluble marriage cases. For the entire work, *see* Orsy, L., et al., "Intolerable Marriage Situations: Conflict between External and Internal Forum," *The Jurist*, 30 (1970) 1-74.

"A Theological Appraisal of Marriage Tribunals," *Divorce and Remarriage in the Catholic Church*, 16-28.

Some of the presuppositions beneath current Church procedures are explored, such as marriage as a contract or covenant, the role of law, and the favor of the law which marriage enjoys. Häring proposes careful consideration of *oikonomia*. *See* CLSA Committee on Tribunal Decision Making.

Harman, Francis, "Statement by the C.L.S.A. on the Revision of the Code and a Commentary," *Canon Law Society of Great Britain and Ireland Newsletter*, 36 (March, 1978) 5-6 and 49-57.

The author agrees with the criticisms offered by the CLSA in its 1977 statement at Houston but he disagrees with its proposals. *See* CLSA, "Statement Concerning the Revision of the Code of Canon Law."

Hartford, Archdiocese of, *see* Lynch, T., "Teenage Marriages and Diocesan Norms Seminar."

Hedderman, John, "The Permanent Diaconate: Its Development and its Canonical Implications," '78 *Proceedings*, 109-116. (*Also, Origins*, v. 8, 300-304.)

Following a presentation of the history of the Permanent Diaconate, the author addresses current criticisms of the institution. He sees the ministry of the Permanent Deacon as both liturgical and pastoral, a ministry of service. The proposed Code does not adequately consider this clerical state and Hedderman challenges canonists to respond to the future development of a growing Permanent Diaconate and all of its possible ramifications.

Hehir, J. Bryan, "The Church in Mission: Canonical Implications," '75 *Proceedings*, 1-11.

Rooting his analysis of the social mission of the Church in *Gaudium et Spes*, the author examines its substance and significance. Hehir then reviews the major trends in Catholic social thought since *Gaudium et*

Spes and concludes by reflecting upon the role of canonists in the light of this Vatican II document and the decade that followed.

Heintschel, Donald, "Participative Leadership and Shared Responsibility in the Church," '72 *Proceedings,* 1-3.

These are the opening remarks and a convention overview presented by the author at the Annual Convention in Seattle, 1972.

"Canon Law Society of America," *New Catholic Encyclopedia,* v. 17, 69-71.

A brief history of the Society.

"A New Code: A Mandate for CLSA's Tomorrow," '80 *Proceedings,* 4-13.

This is the key-note address to the 1980 CLSA Convention and reviews some of the past work of the Society as well as the outgoing Executive-Coordinator's vision for where the Society could develop in the future.

Hennesey, James, "The American Church and Church Law," *Law for Liberty,* 77-84.

Hennesey explores the history of the Catholic Church in the United States to find roots for current renewal in relationships with Rome, Church-State relations, collegiality, lay involvement, the election of bishops, the status of pastors, and interfaith relations. *See* CLSA Symposia, *The Role of Law in the Church.*

"Papal Diplomacy and the Contemporary Church," *The Once & Future Church,* 170-204.

Despite predictions, the number of papal diplomats increased rather than dropped off after the Second Vatican Council. Hennesey explores the implications of this for collegiality, episcopal conferences, and Church-State relations. *See* CLSA Symposia, *Unity and Subsidiarity in the Church.*

Hern, Kevin, "A Positive Approach from Civil Law," *Divorce and Remarriage in the Catholic Church,* 114-120.

After sketching the traditional civil law approach to divorce, Hern explores possible implications from the California experiment with no-fault divorce laws. *See* CLSA Committee on Tribunal Decision Making.

Hess, Hamilton, "The Early Expression of Ecclesiastical Authority and Its Development," *Law for Liberty,* 29-37.

The history of the development of ecclesiastical authority and the role of law in the Church from the second to fifth centuries is the focus of this brief study in an early CLSA symposium. *See* CLSA Symposia, *The Role of Law in the Church.*

"Authority: Its Source, Nature and Purpose in the Church," *We, The People of God . . .*, 131-144.

The charismatic and institutional sources of authority are explored in the context of scripture and the history of the early Church to illustrate the nature and purpose of authority in the Church even today. *See* CLSA Symposia, *A Constitution for the Church.*

"Ecclesial Rights in the Early Christian Community: A Theological Study," *The Case for Freedom: Human Rights in the Church*, 47-75.

In the context of diversity of functions in the early Church, various rights of various people within the community are explored, as well as the erosion of those rights and the gradual centralization of power. *See* CLSA Symposia, *Rights in the Church.*

"Changing Forms of Ministry in the Early Church," *Sexism and Church Law*, 43-57.

The changing structures in the Christian community and changing forms of ministry through the fourth century are studied with a view to the impact these had on the role of women in ministry. *See* CLSA Symposia, *Women and Church Law.*

Heston, Edward, "Present Organizational Design and Structure of the Roman Catholic Church," *We, The People of God . . .*, 29-47.

The basic organizational design of the Church from the Pope and bishops through the Roman Curia, episcopal conferences and the Code of Canon Law is described in a straight-forward manner. *See* CLSA Symposia, *A Constitution for the Church.*

Hierarchy, *see* Orsy, L., "Hierarchy and Religious: Responsibilities, Rights and Duties."

Higgins, John W., "Psychological Influence on the Marriage Bond," *The Bond of Marriage*, 205-218.

Dr. Higgins explores influences of psychological illness and of human needs on the marriage relationship. *See* CLSA Symposia, *The Bond of Marriage.*

Hill, Richard A., "Religious," *The Pastoral Guide to Canon Law*, 316-329.

The developments of renewal in religious life are spelled out in terms of conciliar and post-conciliar rules, as well as the practice of American

58

religious communities. *See* CLSA Committee on Continuing Education.

"Canon Law After Vatican II: Renewal or Retreat," *America*, 137/14 (Nov. 6, 1977) 298-300.

The author critiques the Code Commission and the process employed in the revision of the Code.

& Golden, Paul, "Report on Survey of Teachers of Canon Law." '78 *Proceedings*, 117-124.

Himes, Michael J., "The Current State of Sacramental Theology as a Background to the New Code," '80 *Proceedings*, 60-77.

Developments in sacramental theology are used to evaluate how effectively the new Code will meet the theological and pastoral situation of the Church today.

History, *see*

Bassett, W., "The Marriage of Christians: Valid Contract, Valid Sacrament?"

Burghardt, W., "Church Structure: A Theologian Reflects on History."

Constantelos, D., "Marriage and Celibacy of the Clergy in the Orthodox Church."

Hennesey, J., "The American Church and Church Law."

Hess, H., "Authority: Its Source, Nature and Purpose in the Church."

Hess, H., "Changing Forms of Ministry in the Early Church."

Hess, H., "The Early Expression of Ecclesiastical Authority and Its Development."

Hess, H., "Ecclesiastical Rights in the Early Christian Community: A Theological Study."

Lynch, J., "Critique of the Law of Celibacy in the Catholic Church from the Period of the Reform Councils."

Lynch, J., "Marriage and Celibacy of the Clergy: The Discipline of the Western Church:An Historico-Canonical Synopsis."

Noonan, J., "Freedom, Experimentation, and Permanence in the Canon Law on Marriage."

Noonan, J., "Novel 22."

Noonan, J., "Ursa's Case."

O'Dea, T., "Authority and Freedom in the Church: Tension, Balance and Contradiction: An Historico-Sociological View."

O'Meara, T., "Emergence and Decline of Popular Voice in the Selection of Bishops."

Ozment, S., "Marriage and the Ministry in the Protestant Churches."

Ryan, J.J., "Canon Law in the Gregorian Reform Epoch (c. 1050-1125): Historical Perspectives in the Present Age of Renewal."

Schmemann, A., "The Indissolubility of Marriage: The Theological Tradition of the East."

Sloyan, G., "Biblical and Patristic Motives for Celibacy of Church Ministers."

Stanley, D., "Discerning the Permanent and Transitory: The Experience of the Apostolic Church."

Stern, R., "How Priests came to be Celibate: An Oversimplification."

Tierney, B., "Roots of Western Constitutionalism."

Trisco, R., "The Variety of Procedures in Modern History."

Historical Mindedness, *see*

Alesandro, J., "The Revision of Church Law: Conflict and Reconciliation."

Burghardt, W., "Church Structure: A Theologian Reflects on History."

Lonergan, B., "The Transition from a Classicist World-View to Historical Mindedness."

Hite, Jordan, *see* O'Connor, D. et al., "Current Issues in Religious Law."

Holy Orders, *see* Orders, Holy.

Houston, *see* CLSA, *Proceedings of the Thirty-Ninth Annual Convention, Houston, Texas, 1977.*

Huizing, Peter, "The Structure of Episcopal Conferences," *The Jurist,* 28 (1968) 163-175.

This paper was presented at the Twenty-Ninth Annual Meeting in Denver in 1967. The author examines the structure and the present norms for episcopal conferences in the common law of the Latin Church. Huizing discusses their power and their relationship to councils and synods.

"Law, Conscience, and Marriage," *The Jurist,* 30 (1970) 15-20.

This paper is a part of the report of the *ad hoc* Committee appointed by the CLSA to investigate immediate internal forum solutions for deserving persons involved in canonically insoluble marriage cases. For the entire work, *see* Orsy, L., et al. "Intolerable Marriage Situations: Conflict between External and Internal Forum," *The Jurist*, 30 (1970) 1-74.

"The Indissolubility of Marriage and Church Order," in *The Sacraments in Theology and Canon Law*, *Concilium*, vol. 38, New York, N.Y., Paulist Press, 1968, 45-57.

This article is a review of the CLSA's third symposium, *The Bond of Marriage*.

Human Freedom, *see* Warwick, D., "Human Freedom and the Church of the Future."

Human Rights, *see* Coriden, J., ed., *The Case for Freedom: Human Rights in the Church*.

Hynous, David, "Theology of Participative Leadership," '72 *Proceedings*, 83-85.

This is a brief seminar discussion on the nature, function and limits of authority.

"Challenges to Religious Life—The New Norms for Religious," '75 *Proceedings*, 94-100.

The author discusses the definition, development and living of religious life. These are challenges, he states, not only institutionally within the context of the law, but personally on the part of those who lead in this consecrated way of life and on those who share in this leadership.

-I-

Incapacity, Relative, *see*

Bauer, F., "Relative Incapacity to Establish a Christian Conjugal Union."

Lesage, G., "Relative Incapacity and Invalidity of Marriage."

Incompatibility, *see* Braceland, F., "Psychoneurotic Interpersonal Reaction: Incompatibility and the Tribunal."

Indissolubility, *see* Marriage Indissolubility.

Institutes of Life, *see*

Benson, R., "Election by Community and Chapter: Reflection on Co-responsibility in the Historical Church."

Borgia, F., "Recent Experiences in Religious Renewal."

Boyle, P., ed., *Selected Passages from Religious Constitutions Dealing with the Evangelical Counsels and Community Life.*

Brennan, M., "Standing in Experience: A Reflection on the Status of Women in the Church."

CLSA Workshop on *Community Life and Experimentation.*

Gokey, R., "The Relationship of Religious to the Local Church."

Hill, R., "Religious."

Hynous, D., "Challenges to Religious Life—The New Norms for Religious."

McDermott, R., "Schema of Canons on Institutes of Life Consecrated by Profession of the Evangelical Counsels: Revision or Update?"

Morrisey, F., "The Conveyance of Ecclesiastical Goods."

O'Connor, D., et al., "Current Issues in Religious Law."

O'Connor, D., "Guidelines and Practical Issues in the Drafting of New Constitutions."

O'Rourke, K., "The New Instruction on Formation of Religious."

O'Rourke, K., "The New Law for Religious: Principles, Content and Evaluation."

O'Rourke, K., *Renewal Through Community and Experimentation.*

Orsy, L., "Hierarchy and Religious: Responsibilities, Rights and Duties."

Pennington, M.B., "The Structure of the Section Concerning Religious Life in the Revised Code."

Regan, C., "The Schema of Canons on Institutes of Life Consecrated by Profession of the Evangelical Counsels."

Thomas, B., "Models of Governance for Religious."

Thomas, B., "Participative Leadership in Religious Life.'

Voegtle, L., "Report on Religious Seminar."

See also, CLSA and Religious.

Institutional Change, *see*

Fontinell, E., "Authority and Freedom in the Christian Community, Expressed in the Structures of the Institution."

Meyer, B., "The Perennial Problem of the Church: Institutional Change."

O'Meara, T., "Optional Ministerial Celibacy: Its Effect on Religious Life."

O'Meara, T., "Theological Reflections on Institutional Renewal in the Church."

Intention, Implicit, *see* Brown, R., "Non-inclusion: A Form of Simulation."

Intercommunion, *see*

Bauer, N., "Intercommunion: Possibilities and Practicalities."

Bevilacqua, A., "Problem Areas in Chancery Practice."

Buckley, F., "The Right to the Sacraments of Initiation."

Internal Forum, *see*

Green, T., "Canonical-Pastoral Reflections on Divorce and Remarriage."

Orsy, L., et al., "Intolerable Marriage Situations: Conflicts between External and Internal Forum."

Thrasher, R., "Reflections on Canon 1014."

-J-

Janicki, Joseph, "Limited Term of Office and Retirement," '79 *Proceedings*, 39-59.

The author studies the American experience of limited term of office for pastors. He asks if it is reasonable. What legal means can effect it? Is retirement the ultimate limit? Should limited tenure include other ecclesiastical offices? A chart is included which examines the practice in various dioceses in the U.S.

Jegen, Carol, "Theological Consideration on the Problematic of Permanent Commitment," '70 *Proceedings*, 80-87.

The author reflects on the "God of the hope theologians" and perceives him as the God of promise, a God who is faithful to his promises. Thus, she says, when a promise is understood as a word of love, there is a different perspective to the question—a perspective of forever. A series of questions for discussion purposes concludes her presentation. This paper is part of a workshop jointly presented by Carol Jegen and Richard Westly (q.v.).

"Worship and *Missio*," *The Jurist*, 39 (1979) 88-118.

Jegen searches new forms and old for liturgical contact with the paschal mystery in which the kenotic agape of Christ expresses and empowers the fundamental *missio* which is Church. *See* CLSA Permanent Seminar.

Juridical Status, *see* Morrisey, F., "The Juridical Status of Women in Contemporary Church Law."

Jurisdiction, *see*

Cuneo, J., "The Power of Jurisdiction: Empowerment for Church Functioning and Mission Distinct from the Power of Orders."

Meagher, K., "Women in Relation to Orders and Jurisdiction."

Pelikan, J., "Law and Dogma: Some Historical Interrelations."

Jurisprudence, *see*

Boyle, P., *American Jurisprudence.*

Brossard, A., "Role of the Advocate in the Development of Jurisprudence."

Brown, R., "The Development of Local Jurisprudence."

CLSA, *Matrimonial Jurisprudence, United States.*

Lavin, M., "The Rotal Decision Before Serrano, April 5, 1973: Some Observations Concerning Jurisprudence, Procedure, and Risk."

Maida, A., ed., *The Tribunal Reporter.*

Reinhardt, M., "*Error Qualitatis in Errorem Personae Redundans.*"

Wrenn, L., *Decisions.*

Justice, *see*

Coleman, J., "The Mission of the Church and Action on Behalf of Justice."

Francis, J., "The Canonists—Advocate."

Logar, W., "Liberty and Justice for All: An Ecclesial Interpretation."

Provost, J., "Tribunal Future Shock: Alternatives for Justice."

-K-

Keating, J. Richard, "Sociopathic Personality," *The Jurist*, 25 (1965) 429-438.

This paper was given at the Mid-West Regional Meeting in Indianapolis in 1965. The author analyzes the practice and jurisprudence of the Roman Rota in regard to the inability of the sociopath to give sufficient consent to marriage and the current development of the concept of "moral impotence" as it relates to the psychopathic personality. Keating believes that it is an invalidating disability. (In *The Jurist*, 26 [1966] 266, there is an apology for publishing this talk without the knowledge or consent of the author.)

Kelleher, Stephen, "Canon 1014 and American Culture," *The Jurist*, 28 (1968) 1-12.

This paper was given at the Twenty-Ninth Annual Meeting at Denver in 1967. The author discusses the imperfections and defects of the law and the Tribunal. He calls for a revision of the presumption of c. 1014 so that a marriage could be declared invalid if the more probable arguments favor invalidity and these more probable arguments can be based solely on the statements of the parties. Our juridical system is in error, Kelleher believes, because it is more concerned with protecting the stability of an "institution" rather than safeguarding the rights of human persons in that institution. He concludes with a call for a revision of the present ecclesiastical annulment system and the granting of ecclesiastical divorces even in the case of a sacramental, consummated marriage.

Kennedy, Eugene C., "Signs of Life in Marriage," *Divorce and Remarriage in the Catholic Church*, 121-133.

From a psychological point of view, Kennedy sketches various signs of life which pastoral ministers and tribunal officials should consider when approaching individual marriages. *See* CLSA Committee on Tribunal Decision Making.

Kennedy, Robert T., "Canonical Tradition and Christian Rights," *The Case for Freedom: Human Rights in the Church*, 91-106.

The various rights directly and indirectly expressed in the current Code of Canon Law are analyzed with a view to illustrating the tradition for rights which is contained within the canon law. *See* CLSA Symposia, *Rights in the Church*.

et al., "Report of the *Ad Hoc* Committee on Due Process to the Canon Law Society of America," '69 *Proceedings*, 18-51.

Following a preamble expressing the common rights and freedoms of all persons in the Church, an explanation of the notion of due process is given along with its ecclesiological implications and its governmental context. Processes for conciliation, arbitration and adjudication are given in detail. *See* CLSA, *On Due Process*, and *The Jurist*, 32 (1972) 291-292.

"Address on Due Process to the National Conference of Catholic Bishops," '69 *Proceedings*, 10-17.

The author explains the meaning of due process and how the introduction of notions of due process into the administrative life of the Church can bring about structures and procedures that can provide an assurance of fairness in decision making. He explains the workings of the three-fold structure of conciliation, arbitration and adjudication, and how they are basically rooted in the tradition of the 1917 Code. Kennedy concludes with a discussion on the structuring of administrative discretion and the creation of an atmosphere of Christian living in which disputes are less likely to arise.

ed., *On Due Process*, Hartford, CT, CLSA, 1970.

This work is also known as *Due Process: Blueprint for Procedural Fairness in the Church.* It contains the material contained in a plan for due process prepared by the CLSA and approved by both the NCCB and the Holy See.

"Introductory Address," '71 *Proceedings*, 1-10.

In a call to education in Church government, Kennedy suggests a new emphasis in the work of the CLSA, to make Church government more learned and to serve the broader governmental life of the Church.

"Administrative Law; New Proposed Roman Norms," '72 *Proceedings*, 98-103.

The author offers a favorable critique of the schema of canons on administrative procedure. He says that they show a genuine effort to protect and promote more adequately personal rights within the Church.

"The Early Republic's Challenge to Catholic Church Governance: Bicentennial Reflections of an American Canonist," '76 *Proceedings*, 1-18.

The author suggests the legitimacy of borrowing from American Law in order to serve the Church. He initiates a search into American political theory for elements of governance which are better able to give expression to the ecclesiology of Vatican II. Kennedy calls for a concentrated study of other aspects of American Law and government which can provide further insights with which to enrich the Church's own internal governance.

Kilmartin, Edward J., "Full Participation of Women in the Life of the Catholic Church," *Sexism and Church Law*, 109-135.

The official position is described and evaluated in light of its ecumenical impact. Kilmartin then evaluates the theological argument against the ordination of women, and explores the theological significance of pastoral responsibility currently given to women. *See* CLSA Symposia, *Women and Church Law*.

Kinney, John F., "Rights and Duties of the Faithful in the Schema 'People of God': An Encouragement to Exercise Them," '80 *Proceedings*, 107-114.

This Convention seminar was designed as a process, with the material in *Proceedings* giving the introduction to the process. An appendix gives the rights listed in the earlier version of the schema.

Knox, L. Mason, "Marriage and Ministry: Some Ecumenical Reflections," *The Jurist*, 32 (1972) 463-478.

This paper was given at the Eastern Regional Meeting at Scranton in 1972. The author, an Episcopalian priest canonist, examines Christian marriage and Christian ministry with a canonical concern for avoiding rapid pastoral restructuring at a time when the churches are reconsidering and renewing the law in these areas.

Koinōnia, see

Bissonnette, T., "*Communidades ecclesiales de base*: Some Contemporary Attempts to Build Ecclesial *Koinōnia*."

Prusak, B., "Hospitality Extended or Denied: *Koinōnia* Incarnate from Jesus to Augustine."

Komonchak, Joseph A., "A New Law for the People of God: Some Theological Reflections," '80 *Proceedings*, 14-43.

Analyzing drafts for the *Lex Fundamentalis* and the Schema for Book II, theologian Komonchak raises questions as to how adequate the proposed law is in light of the teaching of Vatican II.

Kosnik, Anthony, "The Pastoral Care of Those Involved in Canonically Invalid Marriages," *The Jurist*, 30 (1970) 31-44.

This is a part of the report of the *ad hoc* Committee apponted by the CLSA to investigate immediate internal forum solutions for deserving persons involved in canonically insoluble marriage cases. For the entire work, *see* Orsy, L., et al., "Intolerable marriage Situations: Conflict between External and Internal Forum," *The Jurist*, 30 (1970) 1-74.

Kress, Robert, "The Church as *Communio*: Trinity and Incarnation as the Foundation of Ecclesiology," *The Jurist*, 36 (1976) 127-158.

The author re-examines the patristic insight into the life of the Trinity as a "dancing together" and applies this ontology to the Church where Christian life is the indwelling of the Trinity. Kress perceives the Church as a communion at various levels and degrees of realization, a unity in diversty. *See* CLSA Permanent Seminar.

-L-

LaDue, William, et al., "A General Analysis of the Proposed Schema on the *Lex Fundamentalis*," '70 *Proceedings*, 29-46. (*Also, The Jurist*, 31 [1971] 342-362.)

The chairman of the CLSA Committee on the *Lex Fundamentalis* offers an evaluation and critique of the schema, together with an analysis of observations on its contents. The Committee concludes that the *Lex* is not acceptable. A new schema should be formulated either through an extraordinary session of the Synod of Bishops or through an expanded committee of consultors made up of bishops, canonists, theologians and representatives of the People of God from all parts of the world.

et al., "A Critique of the Revised Schema on the *Lex Fundamentalis*," '71 *Proceedings*, 65-77.

This is a follow-up on the initial report to the 1970 convention of the CLSA (*see above*) critiquing a revision of the first schema, with more attention to the larger question of the meaning, advisability and feasibility of a document such as the *Lex Fundamentalis*.

"*Causas Matrimoniales* and the American Procedural Norms—A Comparison," '73 *Proceedings*, 112-120. (*Also, Origins*, v. 4, 54-46.)

This paper compares the three innovations of *Causas Matrimoniales* with the parallel dispositions of the APN.

"The Sacramentality of Marriage," '74 *Proceedings*, 25-35.

The author raises the question, does c. 1012, §2 (the contract and the sacrament for the baptized are one) represent an irreformable position of the Church? Following an overview of the history of marriage as sacrament, LaDue concludes that the answer must be "no." He calls for a redefinition of sacramental marriage through a reinterpretation of the distinction between marriage as an *officium naturae* and as a sacrament of the New Law.

Laicization of Priests, *see*

Bevilacqua, A., "Problem Areas in Chancery Practice."

CLSA, "Dispensed Priests in Ecclesial Ministry: A Canonical Reflection."

Laity, *see*

Benson, R., "Election by Community and Chapter: Reflection on Co-responsibility in the Historical Church."

Bourke, M., "Collegial Decision Making in the New Testament."

Brown, E.K., "Co-responsibility in Church Governance: Some Protestant Experiences."

Morrissey, M., "Issues in Chancery Practice."

Landini, Lawrence, "Baptismal Practices in Catholic Hospitals: A Theological Reflection on Canons 752 and 750," *The Jurist,* 35 (1975) 296-309.

This paper was given at the Midwest Regional Convention in 1974. The author examines the theology behind the interpretations of the canons concerning the baptism of an unconscious dying adult and the baptism of a dying infant despite parental objections. Landini discusses past and recent magisterial teaching and concludes with reasons why he believes that these practices should be generally discouraged.

Lasch, Kenneth, *see* CLSA, "Dispensed Priests in Ecclesial Ministry: A Canonical Reflection."

Lavin, Martin, "The Rotal Decision Before Serrano, April 5, 1973: Some Observations Concerning Jurisprudence, Procedure, and Risk," *The Jurist,* 36 (1976) 302-316.

This paper was given at the Eastern Regional Meeting in Pittsburgh in 1975. The author studies Rotal Judge Serrano's much discussed decision regarding "incapacity for interpersonal conjugal consent." Learning from Serrano's contribution to the jurisprudential realm, Lavin concludes that more emphasis must be placed on the habitual ability of the party or parties to relate to another person. Tribunals must investigate, Lavin says, the process of this relationship from beginning to end.

Law, Bernard, "Ecumenism in U.S.A.—Problems and Prospects," '69 *Proceedings,* 129-131.

This is a brief seminar on some of the factors influencing the present and immediate future of the Catholic Church's involvement in the ecumenical movement.

Law and Conscience, *see* Curran, C., "Law and Conscience in the Christian Context."

Law for Liberty, The Role of Law in the Church Today, see Biechler, J., ed.; CLSA Symposia, *The Role of Law in the Church.*

Law, Definition of, *see*

Bourke, V., "The Analogy of Law."

Crosson, F., "Liberty and Authority in the Church."

Law, Procedural, *see* Procedural Law.

Leadership, *see*

Bradburn, N., "Reflections on the Socio-Psychological Dimensions of Leadership and Some Possible Applications to the Church."

Dillon, R., "Theory and Norms of the Governing Ministry Derived from the Gospel of St. Matthew."

Dreher, J., "New Wineskins for New Wine. The Need for Pastoral Planning and Leadership Development for a Church in Transition."

Ellis, J.T., "Those Called to Lead—Then and Now."

Greeley, A., "Leadership and Friendship: A Sociologist's Viewpoint."

Heintschel, D., "Participative Leadership and Shared Responsibility in the Church."

Hynous, D., "Challenges to Religious Life—The New Norms for Religious."

Hynous, D., "Theology of Participative Leadership."

O'Hanlon, D., "The Nature, Extent and Style of Authority in the Church."

Thomas, B., "Participative Leadrship in Religious Life."

Warwick, D., "Personal and Organizational Effectiveness in the Roman Catholic Church."

Leahy, William K., "References to Episcopal Conferences in Conciliar and Other Related Documents," *The Once & Future Church*, 277-299.

In an appendix to this CLSA symposium, Leahy pulls together the various references to episcopal conferences in official Church documents which had appeared up until the end of the Second Vatican Council. *See* CLSA Symposia, *Unity and Subsidiarity in the Church.*

Lecari, Ronald, *see* Doyle, T., & Lecari, R., " 'Everything You Ever Wanted to Know About the Competent Forum But Were Afraid to Ask.' "

Lesage, Germain, "Relative Incapacity and Invalidity of Marriage," '79 *Proceedings,* 76-82.

The psychological nature and import of incapacity and invalidity are discussed by Lesage as to the meaning of the terms, the ambiguity of the expression "relative incapacity," the requirements for a psychological, interpersonal and conjugal relationship, and the canonical grounds for invalidity. Lesage offers concise conclusions.

Lex Fundamentalis, see

Komonchak, J., "A New Law for the People of God: Some Theological Reflections."

LaDue, W., "A General Analysis of the Proposed Schema on the *Lex Fundamentalis.*"

LaDue, W., "A Critique of the Revised Schema of the *Lex Fundamentalis.*"

Liberty, *see* Crosson, F., "Liberty and Authority in the Church."

Littell, Franklin, "The Service of Structures to the Church," *The Jurist,* 28 (1968) 13-22.

This paper was given at the Twenty-Ninth Annual Meeting at Denver in 1967. The author speaks of the necessity of structures in the Church and the need to appraise them by prayerful, lively and continuing reference to Scripture, by careful attention to the natural order and its creatures, and by lively dialogue with the past and the present.

Liturgical Law, *see* Miller, J., "Liturgical Law: Its Nature and Purpose, Its Development and Interpretation."

The Living Light, *see* CLSA, Committee on Continuing Education.

Logar, William, "Minorities Before the Law," *The Jurist,* 39 (1979) 471-480.

In this paper, given at the Western Regional Meeting at Las Vegas in 1979, the author reflects upon the status of minorities within the Church structure, the faith community, and in tribunals. Logar warns of the danger of canonists concentrating so much on tribunals that they may forget the question of justice in the much wider dimension.

"Liberty and Justice for All: An Ecclesial Interpretation," '79 *Proceedings,* 24-31.

The author states that the Church has discriminated against people of different cultural backgrounds and still does. He offers as an example our Eastern Rite brothers and sisters. Logar examines the implications of this in tribunals and in our attitudes toward marriage and family, in Church life in general.

Lonergan, Bernard, "The Transition from a Classicist World View to Historical Mindedness," *Law for Liberty*, 126-133.

One approach to reality is to seek what is unchanging and permanent in human nature; the other is to look for people as they are, and to understand them in their uniqueness. The relative emphasis given to either of these two perspectives tends to result in different world views. Lonergan explores these, contrasting them in terms of theological method as well as the life of people in the Church today. *See* CLSA Symposia, *The Role of Law in the Church.*

See also, J. Alesandro, "The Revision of Church Law: Conflict and Reconciliation."

Lonsway, Francis, "The Case Study Method of Teaching Canon Law," '77 *Proceedings*, 94-97.

The author offers a brief outline of resources, strengths and weaknesses of this method.

Lopez, Felix, "Performance Evaluation for Pastors," '71 *Proceedings*, 55-61.

In this seminar, the author studies the reasons for failure of evaluation programs and then offers the requirements necessary for a successful performance evaluation program.

Love, Conjugal, *see* Crowley, P. & P., "The Meaning of Conjugal Love."

Lucas, John, "The Role of the Tribunal in Second Marriages: The Prohibition," '77 *Proceedings*, 30-48.

The author investigates the 1976 policy of the Archdiocese of Chicago which questions unlimited use of the prohibition (*vetitum*) except in cases where there is certainly a just cause and a possibility of the prohibition having some effect on the parties concerned. Lucas offers an analysis of the prohibition, studying some current practices and explaining Chicago's distinction between a prohibition (*vetitum*) and a recommendation, viz., a pastoral concern for the well-being of the individual involved and his or her projected spouse. The former has a juridic effect while the latter does not. He concludes that the former should be used rarely and the latter more often.

Luther, Martin, *see* McNally, R., "The Roman Process of Martin Luther: A Failure in Subsidiarity."

Lutherans, *see*

Bridston, K., "The Polity and Politics of Church Unity."

See also Ecumenism.

Lynch, John, "Canon Law Society of America," *New Catholic Encyclopedia*, v. 16, 47-48.

This is a brief history of the Society.

"Some Landmarks in the Development of Papal Reservations up to 1400 A.D.," *The Jurist*, 30 (1970) 145-181. [Also published as "The History of Centralization: Papal Reservations," *The Once & Future Church*, 57-109.]

This paper was presented at the 1969 CLSA symposium *Unity and Subsidiarity in the Church: Rome and the Conference of Bishops.* In a study of papal leadership and practices such as censures, dispensations, provisions and the appointment of bishops, the author traces the gradual concentration of power in the hands of the papacy from the primitive local communities of apostolic times to the centralized bureaucracy of Avignon. *See* CLSA Symposia, *Unity and Subsidiarity in the Church.*

"Co-responsibility in the First Five Centuries: Presbyteral Colleges and the Election of Bishops," *The Jurist*, 31 (1971) 14-53.

From the perspective of the presbyteral college and of the process by which Church leaders, especially bishops, were chosen, Lynch studies the exercise of responsibility at the level of the local Church from the period immediately after the New Testament up to the middle of the sixth century. *See* CLSA Symposia, *Co-responsibility in the Church.*

"Marriage and Celibacy of the Clergy, The Discipline of the Western Church: An Historico-Canonical Synopsis," *The Jurist*, 32 (1972): 14-38, 189-212.

A very thorough discussion of the history of the development of the law of celibacy is provided as part of the materials developed for the 1971 CLSA Symposium on priestly celibacy. See CLSA Symposia, *The Future Discipline of Priestly Celibacy.*

"Critique of the Law of Celibacy in the Catholic Church from the Period of the Reform Councils," *Celibacy in the Church*, 57-75.

Celibacy has been a disputed issue in the Church at various times, often marked by efforts at reform. Lynch reviews the debates from before

Trent until the end of the nineteenth century. *See* CLSA Symposia, *The Future Discipline of Priestly Celibacy.* This article is an abbreviation of the study published in *The Jurist* (*see above*).

"Ecumenical Marriages," '73 *Proceedings,* 33-54.

On the basis of a survey he has concluded, the author studies the striking changes that have occured since Vatican II and the enormous increase in the number of mixed marriages. He considers the effect that this has had on the Church in the U.S. Lynch then discusses how Church law has been implemented in other countries and the Protestant reaction to the new Church law. He concludes with a reflection on the joint pastoral care mandated by *Matrimonia mixta.*

"The Limits of *Communio* in the Pre-Constantinian Church," *The Jurist,* 36 (1976) 159-190.

The author examines excommunication as seen as a severance from full communion in the life of the Church. Lynch demonstrates how the living practice of Christian communities before Constantine eventually developed a uniform discipline of excommunication. *See* CLSA Permanent Seminar.

"Ecumenical Guidelines," *The Pastoral Guide to Canon Law,* 330-348.

The approach to ecumenism as it has developed through the Second Vatican Council and in post-conciliar directives is detailed in question and answer format. *See* CLSA Committee on Continuing Education.

Lynch, Thomas, "Teenage Marriages and Diocesan Norms," '72 *Proceedings,* 62-69.

In this seminar the author explains the pluses and minuses of the policy of the Archdiocese of Hartford, together with the facts and the problems and some principles for a solution.

"Implementation of Past C.L.S.A. Research in the Area of Marriage," '73 *Proceedings,* 13-16.

The author presents a brief resumé of projects over the past decade undertaken by the CLSA such as the 1967 symposium on *The Bond of Marriage,* studies on "The Good Faith Case" and "The Internal Forum Solution," as well as "The Privilege of the Faith Case" and research on preparation for marriage, specifically the marriages of the very young.

The "Twenty-Three Norms" approved by Rome resulted from the Society's construction of a positive model of procedural law, Lynch points out, and publiction of *Divorce and Remarriage in the Catholic Church* resulted from interdisciplinary studies on decision making in matrimonial cases.

Lynch states that research studies were done with the advent of *Matrimonia mixta* in 1970 and a study was done on the streamlining of the process for non-consummation cases. The Society's model report was approved by the Apostolic Signatura.

He concludes by pointing to Fr. Lawrence Wrenn's work, *Annulments*, which was the result of the Society's need for a clear, concise, comprehensive outline of the best jurisprudence. *The Tribunal Reporter* was the work of a committee of the CLSA, chaired by Fr. Adam Maida, and it was followed by *Matrimonial Jurisprudence: United States, 1968-1971*, edited by Fr. John Dolciamore.

-M-

MacRae, George W., "Freedoms and Rights of the Christian: New Testament Foundations," *The Case for Freedom: Human Rights in the Church*, 15-32.

MacRae explores Galatians and First Corinthians to provide the basis for freedoms and rights of Christians in the scriptures. *See* CLSA Symposia, *Rights in the Church*.

"New Testament Perspectives on Marriage and Divorce," *Divorce and Remarriage in the Catholic Church*, 1-15.

A careful exploration of New Testament data reveals the strong position taken by Jesus as well as the exceptions gradually introduced by the early Christian community and enshrined in Scripture. See CLSA Committee on Tribunal Decision Making.

Mahoney, Roger, "Due Process Within the National Conference of Catholic Bishops," '79 *Proceedings*, 19-23.

The author salutes the tenth anniversary of the collaborative efforts of the CLSA and the NCCB in producing the Due Process Guidelines and examines the proposed procedures for the NCCB's Committee on Arbitration. Mahoney calls for the education of persons regarding their rights in the Church and offers his personal views on the direction Due Process will take in the future.

Maida, Adam, ed., *The Tribunal Reporter*, Huntington, IN, Our Sunday Visitor Press, Inc., 1970; 2nd ed. 1973.

This work, together with L. Wrenn's *Annulments*, alerted tribunal personnel and parish priests to the newly recognized grounds for the alleviation of persons who found themselves in situations of failed marriages. The work itself is the result of an extensive study of some of the most significant decisions of ecclesiastical courts in the United States. Sixty-six cases in the areas of total simulation, exclusion of children, permanence and fidelity, force and fear, mental illness and impotence, are analyzed and reviewed. They exemplify the best in American ecclesiastical jurisprudence. For reviews of this work, *see* Morrisey, F., *Studia Canonica*, 4 (1970) 163; Reinhardt, M., *The Jurist*, 30 (1970) 404-408.

"Rights in the Church," *The Pastoral Guide to Canon Law*, 255-268.

In question and answer form, the human rights, ecclesial rights, and special rights of various individuals in the Church are explored. Due process and other means of protecting rights are explained. *See* CLSA Committee on Continuing Education.

"Visionary or Reactionary: The Canonist's Challenge to Create," '77 *Proceedings*, 1-9.

The author calls for more involvement on the part of the canonist in the emerging areas of Church-State relationships, in a broader advocacy role for Church interests, and in good government in the Church. Maida proposes a supportive structure for this increased involvement.

Mallet, James K., "Diocesan Structure and Governance," '80 *Proceedings*, 151-160.

The governance of dioceses under the proposed new law is examined at the diocesan and at the parish level.

Mangan, Martin, *see* Coriden, J. & Mangan, M., "Team Ministry."

Mansfield, John H., "A Bill of Rights for the Church: Relevance of the Anglo-American Experience," *The Case for Freedom: Human Rights in the Church*, 129-163.

Harvard Law Professor Mansfield explores the background of the Bill of Rights for the United States, expressions of rights in other parts of the world, and the situation of the Catholic Church. He explores questions relative to democracy and the Church, substantive freedom, and procedural fairness. *See* CLSA Symposia, *Rights in the Church*.

Marriage, Annotations in Baptismal Register, *see* Bevilacqua, A., "Problem Areas in Chancery Practice."

Marriage of Baptized Non-Believers, *see* Cuenin, W., "The Marriage of Baptized Non-Believers: Questions of Faith, Sacrament and Law."

Marriage, Canonical Bases for Deferral or Refusal of, *see*

Marriage and Favor of the Law, *see*

Carney, R., "New Applications of Canon 1127."

Häring, B., "A Theological Appraisal of Marriage Tribunals."

Kelleher, S., "Canon 1014 and American Culture."

Orsy, L., "An Evaluation of 'New Applications of Canon 1127.' "

Thrasher, R., "Reflections on Canon 1014."

Marriage, Form of, *see*

Bevilacqua, A., "Problem Areas in Chancery Practice."

CLSA Publications, *Simplification of Procedures in Privilege of Faith and Lack of Form Cases.*

Marriage, Indissolubility of, *see*

Bassett, W., ed., *The Bond of Marriage: An Ecumenical and Interdisciplinary Study.*

Finnegan, J., "When is a Marriage Indissoluble? Reflections on a Contemporary Understanding of a Ratified and Consummated Marriage."

McCormick, R., "Indissolubility and the Right to the Eucharist—Separate Issues or One?"

Noonan, J., "Papal Dissolution of Marriage: Fiction and Function."

Wrenn, L., "Marriage—Indissoluble or Fragile?"

Marrige and the Internal Forum, *see*

Orsy, L., et al., "Intolerable Marriage Situtions: Conflict Bewteen External and Internal Forum."

Thrasher, R., "Reflections on Canon 1014."

Marriage and Interpersonal Relationship, *see*

Bourke, V., "Marital Fidelity and Philosophy."

Dolciamore, J., "Interpersonal Relationships and Their Effect on the Validity of Marriages."

Higgins, J., "Psychological Influences on the Marriage Bond."

Marriage, Inter-ritual, *see* Bevilacqua, A., "Problem Areas in Chancery Practice."

Marriage Legislation, *see*

Finnegan, J., "Marriage."

McBrien, Richard P., "Collegiality: State of the Question," *The Once & Future Church*, 1-24.

On the basis of historical and theological studies, McBrien presents ten conclusions synopsizing the state of the question on the meaning and practice of collegiality in the Church today. See CLSA Symposia, *Unity and Subsidiarity in the Church.*

"A Preliminary Ecclesiological Statement," *The Choosing of Bishops*, 11-20.

Four basic themes fundamental to discussing the choosing of bishops are reviewed: the mission of the Church, the People of God, collegiality, and ordained ministry. *See* CLSA Committee on the Selection of Bishops.

McCormick, Richard, "Indissolubility and the Right to the Eucharist— Separate Issues or One?" '75 *Proceedings*, 26-37.

The author defines the issue and offers the positions of those who hold it is a single issue and those who hold there are separate issues. He concludes with personal reflections on a practical public policy of admission of some divorced-remarried persons to the sacraments which does not constitute a challenge to the teaching on indissolubility of marriage and thereby weaken the Church's unity in faith and discipline. That must be made "abundantly clear," says McCormick, and it can be, he believes, for the issues are "separate."

McDaniel, Helen, "A Social Agency Looks at the Family," *Divorce and Remarriage in the Catholic Church*, 89-104.

The director of a diocesan social service agency explores the setting of marriage in the United States today with special attention to changing life styles and new mores. *See* CLSA Committee on Tribunal Decision Making.

McDermott, Rose, A Review of J. Coriden's *Sexism and Church Law, The Jurist*, 40 (1980) 218-221.

"Schema of Canons on Institutes of Life Consecrated by Profession of the Evangelical Counsels: Revision or Update?" '80 *Proceedings*, 124-131.

Working from *Communicationes* reports of the work group developing the 1979-1980 draft, observations are developed concerning structure, terminology, subsidiarity, literary form, and typology.

McDevitt, Anthony, "Report of Committee on Alternatives to Tribunal Procedures," '75 *Proceedings*, 163-178.

The Committee's chairman addresses the issues of admission of divorced and remarried Catholics to the Eucharist and the admission of divorced persons to remarriage in the Church. This report is also referred to as the "McDevitt Report."

McDonald, James & Biechler, James, "New Horizons in Canon Law," *Chicago Studies*, 1 (1965) 53-66.

The authors discuss the deliberations and thinking of the CLSA at the dawn of the post-conciliar era. They say that the new constitutions of the Society tend away from legalism and towards a new spirit of pastoral service. The CLSA, they believe, will make an effective contribution toward the revision of the Code of Canon Law.

McManus, Frederick, "The Scope of Authority of Episcopal Conferences," *The Once & Future Church*, 129-178.

After exploring the history and development of the episcopal conferences, McManus examines their position in the light of the documents of the Second Vatican Council and explores various theories about the kinds of authority they can exercise. *See* CLSA Symposia, *Unity and Subsidiarity in the Church.*

"Role of the Canonist: Interpreter and Advocate," '74 *Proceedings*, 98-105.

In this seminar the interpretative function of the canonist and his advocacy role are discussed as significant ministries in the Church. The author says that they are to be exercised with care and candor, with vision and openness.

A review of the Proceedings of the Thirty-Seventh Annual Convention, CLSA, San Diego, 1975, *The Jurist*, 36 (1976) 260-261.

"The Sacraments of the Church," *The Pastoral Guide to Canon Law*, 349-371.

Developments in the theological understanding of the sacraments as well as legislation on all the sacraments except marriage and orders are set forth in question and answer format. *See* CLSA Committee on Continuing Education.

McNally, Robert E., "The Tridentine Church: A Study in Ecclesiology," *Law for Liberty*, 69-76.

After describing the historical, theological and canonical setting, McNally argues that the key weakness of the Tridentine reform was its failure to bring about a reform in the Roman Curia. *See* CLSA Symposia, *The Role of Law in the Church.*

"The Roman Process of Martin Luther: A Failure in Subsidiarity," *The Once & Future Church*, 111-128.

Examining the historical steps which led to the condemnation of Martin Luther, McNally concludes that an underlying problem in handling the situaton was the altercation between exempt religious and episcopal authority. The case should have been handled at the local level, but was not. *See* CLSA Symposia, *Unity and Subsidiarity in the Church.*

McNeill, John, "The Relevance of Conciliarism," *The Jurist,* 31 (1971) 81-112.

In an era which holds out the promise of Christian unity, the author believes that history can teach us a lesson. McNeill studies the representative government of religious orders together with medieval and Protestant conciliarism, and states that the central concerns of both the medieval and modern conciliarists are relevant to today's desire for a wider collegiality. *See* CLSA Symposia, *Co-responsibility in the Church.*

Meagher, Katherine, "Women in Relation to Orders and Jurisdiction," *Sexism and Church Law,* 21-42.

The history, canonical legislation and current practice on this issue are reviewed in order to identify five issues requiring even further research at a more fundamental level. *See* CLSA Symposia, *Women and Church Law.*

Meyendorff, John, "Historical Relativism and Authority in Christian Dogma," *The Jurist,* 31 (1971) 143-162.

The author, an Orthodox theologian, states that the problem of authority has a long history, especially in East-West relations. In Orthodox theology the "auxiliary" character of authority is stressed. Meyendorff looks to a definition of authority in matters pertaining to the Christian faith by an examination of the problem through history and patristics. *See* CLSA Symposia, *Co-responsibility in the Church.*

Meyer, Ben F., "The Perennial Problem of the Church: Institutional Change," *Law for Liberty,* 119-125.

Using theological analysis based on Saint Thomas Aquinas and the Second Vatican Council, Meyer explores the concept of change in the insitutional Church as well as freedom within the Church. *See* CLSA Symposia, *The Role of Law in the Church.*

Meyer, Charles R., "Christian Freedom," *The Case for Freedom: Human Rights in the Church,* 77-89.

Theologian Meyer argues that the common man has come of age, and that a new framework beyond the scholastic view of freedom is needed to meet this new condition. *See* CLSA Symposia, *Rights in the Church.*

Miller, John, "Liturgical Law: Its Nature and Purpose, Its Development and Interpretation," '74 *Proceedings,* 83-85.

This brief seminar is aimed at clarifying the purpose of liturgical law.

Ministry, *see*

Burghardt, W., "Church Structure: A Theologian Reflects on History."

CLSA, Committee on Continuing Education.

CLSA Symposia, *The Future Discipline of Priestly Celibacy.*

Coriden, J., "Ministry."

Cunningham, A., "Church People as Missionary: A Ministerial Church."

Green, T., "Reflections on the People of God Schema."

Hess, H., "Changing Forms of Ministry in the Early Church."

McBrien, R., "A Preliminary Ecclesiological Statement."

Nardoni, E., "Ministries in the New Testament."

O'Malley, P., "The Canon Law Society of America and the Needs of the Ministry."

Sheets, J., "Ministry, Spirituality and the Canon Lawyer."

Ministry, Family, *see* Conroy, D., "Canonical Challenges in the Pastoral Ministry of Families."

Ministry and Marriage, *see* Knox, L.M., "Marriage and Ministry: Some Ecumenical Reflections."

Ministry and Women, *see*

Bissonnette, R., "Ecclesiastical Ministry and Women."

CLSA Symposia, *Women and Church Law.*

Minorities, *see*

Logar, W., "Liberty and Justice for All: An Ecclesial Interpretation."

Logar, W., "Minorities Before the Law."

Mission, *see*

Borgia, M.F., "Recent Experiences in Religious Renewal."

Cuneo, J., "The Power of Jurisdiction: Empowerment for Church Functioning and Mission Distinct from the Power of Orders."

Cunningham, A., "Church People as Missionary: A Ministerial Church."

Haight, R., "The Established Church as Mission: The Relation of the Church to the Modern World."

Hehir, J.B., "The Church in Mission: Canonical Implications."

Jegen, C., "Worship and *Missio.*"

McBrien, R., "A Preliminary Ecclesiological Statement."

O'Rourke, K., "The New Law for Religious: Principles, Content and Evaluation."

Provost, J., "Structuring the Church as *Missio.*"

Molloy, Thomas, "The Theological Foundation of Ecclesiastical Due Process," '79 *Proceedings,* 60-67.

The author analyzes Due Process in the American Church and examines the future problems and challenges it presents. Molloy states that Due Process must not be simply for the defense of individual rights but must also preserve ecclesiastical communion, the all important network of grace-produced relationships.

Moral Certitude, *see* Burns, D., "Moral Certitude."

Moral Theology, *see*

Curran, C., "Divorce—From the Perspective of Moral Theology."

Curran, C., "Law and Conscience in the Christian Context."

Curran, C., "Responsibility in Moral Theology: Centrality, Foundations and Implications for Ecclesiology."

Häring, B., "A Theological Appraisal of Marriage Tribunals."

van der Poel, C., "Influences of an 'Annulment Mentality.' "

Moreau, Jules, L., "Choosing Bishops in the Anglican Communion," *The Choosing of Bishops,* 74-84.

Various approaches taken to the choosing of bishops in different parts of the world by churches which form the Anglican communion are reviewed. *See* CLSA Committee on the Selection of Bishops.

Morrisey, Francis, A review of A. Maida's *The Tribunal Reporter, Studia Canonica,* 4 (1970) 163.

A review of W. Bassett's *The Choosing of Bishops, Studia Canonica,* 5 (1971) 181.

A review of L. Wrenn's *Divorce and Remarriage in the Catholic Church, Studia Canonica,* 7 (1973) 320-321.

Canonical Significance of Papal and Curial Pronouncements, Hartford, CT, CLSA, 1974.

The author studies the various types of official pronouncements used by the Church. Some are legislative in nature and some simply provide guidelines for good order. In order to understand the intent and purpose of a document, Morrisey analyzes the various types of papal pronouncements, such as the solemn profession of faith, decretals, encyclicals, exhortations, addresses, Apostolic constitutions, *motu proprio,* etc. and then examines the different categories of texts prepared by Roman, diocesan and religious *curiae,* including decrees, instructions, declarations, circular letters, directories, official responses, etc. He also discusses the constitutions, decrees, declarations and messages prepared by the Fathers at the Second Vatican Council.

"Proposed Legislation on Defective Matrimonial Consent," '74 *Proceedings,* 71-82. (*Also, Origins,* v. 4, 321-328.)

After studying some of the proposed changes presented by the Pontifical Commission for the Revision of the Code on the question of defective matrimonial consent, the author points out what will be required for matrimonial consent and some of the practical applications that arise from these proposed changes.

"The Conveyance of Ecclesiastical Goods," '76 *Proceedings,* 123-137.

In 1974 a joint committee was established by the Conference of Major Superiors of Men, the Leadership Conference of Women Religious, and the Canadian Religious Conference to study the concept of conveyance (alienation). The author gives a summary of the report, an explanation of the concepts involved, and some proposed applications for contemporary practice. Morrisey concludes the seminar with an examination of some of the proposed changes in patrimonial law.

"The Role of Canon Law Today," *The Pastoral Guide to Canon Law,* 236-254.

The development of canon law, its role in the Church, and progress toward a reform of the Code are detailed in question and answer form. *See* CLSA Committee on Continuing Education.

"The Current Status of Procedural Law," '78 *Proceedings,* 49-59.

The author presents a history and development of procedural law in the

Church and examines the proposed new procedural law. He concludes by applying his findings to contemporary situations.

"The Spirit of Canon Law: Teachings of Pope Paul VI," *Canon Law Society of Great Britain & Ireland Newsletter*, 38 (September, 1978) 40-56. (*Also, Origins*, v. 8, 33-40.)

In this paper given at the Midwest Regional Meeting at Duluth, Minnesota, in 1978 the author brings together the many talks of Pope Paul VI on Canon Law in the life of the Church. Morrisey points out the pope's emphasis on the sign value of justice, equity and truth, and Paul's conviction that a close relationship between theology and Canon Law is essential if the new Code is to have a more spiritual character, for the law is based on the Gospel.

"The Juridical Status of Women in Contemporary Ecclesial Law," *Sexism and Church Law*, 1-20.

Using Vatican II as the expression of current Church law, Morrisey evaluates the juridical status of women now and as it is proposed under the suggestions for a revision available at the time (1976). *See* CLSA Symposia, *Women and Church Law.*

& Fellhauer, David E., & Alesandro, John A., "Marriage Legislation in the New Code," '80 *Proceedings*, 78-106.

A number of practical implications for canon law and pastoral practice are explored in light of proposed revisions in the new Code.

Morrissey, Michael, "Issues in Chancery Practice," '79 *Proceedings*, 37-38.

The author offers the experiences of a mid-sized, mid-western diocese which raise questions in areas of co-responsibility of the laity. Morrissey presents suggestions on how that can be effected on a working level.

Moudry, James, "Bishop and Priest in the Sacrament of Holy Orders," *The Jurist*, 31 (1971) 163-186.

The author addresses himself to the collegial responsibility of the presbytery. He does this by examining the historical development of the ordination rites in an effort to uncover what the liturgical texts have to contribute to a clearer understanding of the offices of bishop and priest and the relationship between them. *See* CLSA Symposia, *Co-responsibility in the Church.*

Murphy, Thomas J., "Towards a Theology of Marriage," *The Living Light*, 14 (1977) 38-48.

The theology of marriage must be rooted in revelation. Murphy explores the key themes in scripture, their development in the history of the Church, and the experience of married couples today, to develop main directions for a theology of marriage. This study belongs with the special studies in the previous issue of this journal. *See* CLSA, Committee on Continuing Education.

Murray, John Courtney, "Freedom, Authority, Community," *We, The People of God . . .* , 145-157.

Rather than a "crisis" of authority or of freedom, Murray presents the current situation in the Church in terms of a "crisis of community." *See* CLSA Symposia, *A Constitution for the Church.*

-N-

Nardoni, Enrique, "Ministries in the New Testament," *Studia Canonica*, 11 (1977) 5-36.

This paper was presented at the Northwest Regional Meeting in 1977. It is a study of the various ministries during the years 51 to 105 A.D. and how these led to the institution of presbyters, bishops and deacons.

Natale, Samuel, "The Tribunal *Vetitum*: Limit Setting and Confrontation," *Studia Canonica*, 12 (1978) 365-375.

This paper was originally given at the Eastern Regional Meeting in 1978. Rewritten with J.A. Pepe, it addresses the issuing of a *vetitum* and the opportunity for sympathetically confronting a person who is suffering from a character deficiency and is not aware of it. The informed judge can then decide what is the realistic thing to do; i.e., prohibit a second marriage outrightly, or urgently propose that the person obtain counseling.

National Conference of Catholic Bishops, *A Summary of Actions Taken by the NCCB on the Subject of Due Process*, Washington, D.C., NCCB, 1970.

See also CLSA Symposia, *Unity and Subsidiarity in the Church: Rome and the Conference of Bishops.*

Conroy, D., "Canonical Challenges in the Pastoral Ministry of Families."

Kennedy, R., "Address on Due Process to the National Conference of Catholic Bishops."

Mahoney, R., "Due Process Within the National Conference of Catholic Bishops."

National Federation of Priests' Councils, *see*

O'Malley, Patrick, "The Canon Law Society of America and the Needs of the Ministry.

Provost, J., et al., "What Role for Dispensed Priests?"

National Pastoral Council, *see* O'Meara, T., "Theological Reflections on Institutional Renewal in the Church."

New Orleans, *see* CLSA, *Proceedings of the Thirty-Second Annual Convention*, New Orleans, Louisiana, 1970.

New Testament, *see*

Bourke, M., "Collegial Decision-Making in the New Testament."

Crossan, D., "Divorce and Remarriage in the New Testament."

MacRae, G., "New Testament Perspectives on Marriage and Divorce."

Nardoni, E., "Ministries in the New Testament."

Shepherd, M., "The Rights of the Baptized."

Stanley, D., "Discerning the Permanent and Transitory: The Experience of the Apostolic Church."

See also Gospel; Matthew, St.; Scripture and Canon Law.

Noonan, John T., "Freedom, Experimentation, and Permanence in the Canon Law on Marriage," *Law for Liberty*, 52-68.

As an illustration of what is changeable and what is permanent in canon law, Noonan explores changes which have occurred in the canon law on marriage. In general, a distinction can be made between the law on relationships and the law on consent, capacity, and indissolubility. Law on relationships seems to have been subject to much greater change than law on the other topics. *See* CLSA Symposia, *The Role of Law in the Church.*

"Novel 22," *The Bond of Marriage*, 41-90.

Justinian's divorce legislation is set in its cultural, legal and civil-political settings as well as its theological context. *See* CLSA Symposia, *The Bond of Marriage.*

"Papal Dissolution of Marriage: Fiction and Function," '69 *Proceedings*, 89-95.

Following a brief history of the Pope's power over the marriages of unbelievers, the author distinguishes between the legal fictions and the practical functions performed by these fictions. Noonan concludes that the position that marriages are naturally indissoluble seems to be untenable.

"Ursa's Case," *Divorce and Remarriage in the Catholic Church*, 29-41.

In an effort to uncover some of the earliest evidence of Church tribunal procedure for resolving marital cases, Noonan explores a rescript of Pope Innocent I. *See* CLSA Committee on Tribunal Decision Making.

"Abortion on Demand as the Law of the Land," '74 *Proceedings*, 86-97.

The author discusses the legal sequel to the January 22, 1973, Supreme Court decision which declared unconstitutional the statutes of the fifty states on abortion. Noonan cites examples of ineffectual and salvaging responses, and discusses the dynamism of the abortion movement together with the role of lawyers and judges in the promotion of abortion.

-O-

Obedience, *see* Swift, T., "The Human Dimensions of Authority and Obedience in a Faith Community."

O'Callaghan, Michael et al., "Committee Report on Regional Tribunals," '69 *Proceedings*, 143-155.

The findings and proposals of a pre-"American Procedural Norms" Study.

O'Connor, David, "Guidelines and Practical Issues in the Drafting of New Constitutions," '78 *Proceedings*, 74-100.

This is an aid and a direction for religious institutes in drawing up new constitutions based on the 1977 Proposed Schema of Canons on Institutes of Life Consecrated by Profession of the Evangelical Counsels.

et al., "Current Issues in Religious Law," '79 *Proceedings*, 68-75.

The author, together with Jordan Hite and Joseph Galante, presents a panel discussion on poverty, patrimony, civil law, and religious and new institutes.

O'Dea, Thomas, "Authority and Freedom in the Church: Tension, Balance and Contradiction, An Historico-Sociological View," *The Jurist*, 31 (1971) 223-249.

In the belief that the older forms of the "authority-community-tradition" complex are no longer viable as a model of society in our day, the author analyzes the basic elements of institutional authority, ecclesiastical authority, conflict and contradiction among rationality, charism and tradition, and the use of spiritual "force and violence." O'Dea concludes that the Church today must evolve a sacral but flexible authority leaving a certain freedom for charism and recognizing the inviolabilty of reason. *See* CLSA Symposia, *Co-responsibility in the Church.*

O'Hanlon, Daniel J., "The Nature Extent and Style of Authority in the Church," *Law for Liberty*, 109-118.

Basing authority in the Church on the gosepl style of authority illustrated by Christ, O'Hanlon calls for an authority which is simple and unostentatious, is exercised communally, is based upon open communication, personal, with a relaxed style, and exhibiting rare courage when needed. *See* CLSA Symposia, *The Role of Law in the Church.*

O'Malley, Patrick, "The Canon Law Society of America and the Needs of the Ministry," '70 *Proceedings*, 53-59.

The author offers suggestions for the structural changes needed if the Church is not to lose the tremendous energy unleased by the painful process of change. He states that the Canon Law Society of America has responsibly demonstrated the type of professionalism, with personalism, that priests can admire. O'Malley calls for continued advocacy on behalf of priests and laity and a special consideration of the Church of the future and our role in it.

O'Meara, Thomas, "Theological Reflections on Institutional Renewal in the Church," '70 *Proceedings*, 1-14.

The author says that the re-organization of the Church is not a single enterprise, but a lasting task with no immediate end. Critiquing the August 30, 1970 Mundelein Consulation on the advisability of a National Pastoral Council, O'Meara says that he favors such a body as a national assembly to face the problems of the Church in America. "Structural theologians"—canonists included—must look to pastoral restructuring, he states, and he suggests the National Pastoral Council as a model.

"Emergence and Decline of Popular Voice in the Selection of Bishops," *The Choosing of Bishops*, 21-32.

Drawing on recent studies, O'Meara attempts to get behind the historical and biblical data to see the role of local Christian communities in selecting their central office-holders. *See* CLSA Committee on the Selection of Bishops.

"Optional Ministerial Celibacy: Its Effect on Religious Life," *American Ecclesiastical Review*, 166 (1972) 587-596.

Religious life has a distinct impact on the ideals and practice of celibacy even for secular clergy. The history of this development is explored as well as the present situation. *See* CLSA Symposia, *The Future of Priestly Celibacy.*

On Due Process, *see* CLSA Publications; Kennedy, R.

Once & Future Church: A Communion of Freedom, *see* CLSA Symposia, *Unity and Subsidiarity in the Church: Rome and the Conference of Bishops*; Coriden, J., ed.

Orders, Holy, *see*

Cardman, F., "Tradition, Hermeneutics and Ordination."

Green T., et al., "Reflections on Other Parts of the Proposed Draft *De Sacramentis.*"

Moudry, J., "Bishop and Priest in the Sacrament of Holy Orders."

Orders, Power of, *see*

Cuneo, J., "The Power of Jurisdiction: Empowerment for Church Functioning and Mission Distinct from the Power of Orders."

Meagher, K., "Women in Relation to Orders and Jurisdiction."

Organizational Design, *see*

Bassett, W., "Subsidiarity, Order and Freedom in the Church."

Bridston, K., "The Polity and Politics of Church Unity."

Greeley, A., "A Social Organizational View of the Catholic Church."

Gumbleton, T., "The Diocesan Synod in Detroit: Renewal in Process."

Heston, E., "Present Organizational Design and Structure of the Roman Catholic Church."

Provost, J., "Structuring the Community."

Zizola, G., "The Reformed Roman Curia."

Organizational Effectiveness, *see*

Dreher, J., "New Wineskins for New Wine. The Need for Pastoral Planning and Leadership Development for a Church in Transition."

Sexton, W., "A Comparative Examination of the Exercise of Authority in the Church."

Warwick, D., "Personal and Organizational Effectiveness in the Roman Catholic Church."

Oriental Churches, *see*

Constantelos, D., "Marriage and Celibacy of the Clergy in the Orthodox Church."

Dvornik, F., "Origins of Episcopal Synods."

Meyendorff, J., "Historical Relativism and Authority in Christian Dogma."

Schmemann, "The Indissolubility of Marriage: The Theological Tradition of the East."

Wojnar, M., "Participation of the Clergy and Laity in the Election of Bishops According to the Discipline of the Oriental Catholic Churches."

See also Eastern Rites.

Orlando, *see* CLSA, *Proceedings of the Forty-Second Annual Convention*, Orlando, Florida, 1980.

O'Rourke, John, "The Faith Required for the Privilege of the Faith Dispensation," *The Jurist*, 36 (1976) 450-455.

This paper was presented at the Eastern Regional Meeting at Clearwater, Florida, in 1976. It is an exegesis of I Corinthians 7:12-16 and an application of it to cc. 1120-1121.

O'Rourke, Kevin, *Renewal Through Community and Experimentation*, Hartford, CT, CLSA, 1968. *See* CLSA Workshop on *Community Life and Experimentation*.

"The New Instruction on Formation of Religious," '69 *Proceedings*, 102-111.

The author discusses *Renovationis causam* (Instruction on the Renewal of Religious Formation), its prescriptions, legal innovations and questions, and the innovations for the future suggested by the document. O'Rourke believes that because of the document's respect for subsidiarity, experimentation and individual freedom, it augurs well for the future.

"The New Law for Religious: Principles, Content and Evaluation," '74 *Proceedings*, 45-70.

The author evaluates the principles, outline and content of the proposed new canons for institutes of perfection. O'Rourke suggests that greater emphasis needs to be given in concrete terms to the implications of mission to the people of God, and greater consultation must be had with those people who are to be affected most intimately by the new law.

Orsy, Ladislas M., "The Dynamic Spirit of Common Law and the Renewal of Canon Law," *Law for Liberty,* 172-180.

Orsy argues that the current legal system of the Church is not open enough, and points to how taking the common law into account would improve the situation. *See* CLSA Symposia, *The Role of Law in the Church.*

"Quantity and Quality of Laws after Vatican II," *The Jurist,* 27 (1967) 385-412.

This paper was presented at the Midwest Regional Meeting at St. Paul, Minnesota in 1967. The author is concerned with the present and immediate future of the Church's life from the point of view of legislation. Orsy weighs the quantity and evaluates the quality of law while emphasizing the principles that should lead the legislator.

A review of J. Coriden's *We, the People of God . . . A Study of Constitutional Government for the Church, The Jurist,* 29 (1969) 210-215.

et al., "Intolerable Marriage Situations: Conflict between External and Internal Forum," *The Jurist,* 30 (1970) 1-14. (*Also,* '69 *Proceedings,* 56-68.)

In 1968 the CLSA resolved that a special *ad hoc* committee be appointed to investigate immediate internal forum solutions for deserving persons involved in canonically insoluble marriage cases. The committee, chaired by Ladislas Orsy, included James Coriden, Robert Kennedy, John Catoir and Anthony Padovano. Orsy's article is the report of this committee and it, together with papers submitted by theologians, was presented to the 1969 convention of the CLSA. For the entire work, *see The Jurist,* 30 (1970) 1-74.

"Hierarchy and Religious: Responsibilities, Rights and Duties," '77 *Proceedings,* 19-29.

The author presents a foundation on which new legislation can be built through an analysis of the role of the hierarchy and the role of religious in the Church. Orsy examines their individual responsibilities in the service of the whole body and how spiritual and internal obligations are to be translated into legal rights and duties.

"An Evaluation of 'New Applications of Canon 1127,' " *The Jurist,* 38 (1978) 163-170.

This is a response to a paper given by Richard Carney at the CLSA's Annual Convention at Houston in 1977.

Ozment, Steven, "Marriage and the Ministry in the Protestant Churches," *Celibacy in the Church,* 39-56.

Concentrating on the Reformation period itself, the attitude toward marriage for the clergy and its practical implementation by reformation churches are explained. Some modern issues among Protestants are also raised. *See* CLSA Symposia, *The Future Discipline of Priestly Celibacy.*

-P-

Padovano, Anthony, "A Theology of Church Government," '71 *Proceedings,* 23-27.

The author examines the notion of authority and the community-society dialectic. He calls for collegial responsibility in the development of community consciousness.

Papal Diplomacy, *see* Hennesey, J., "Papal Diplomacy and the Contemporary Church."

Papal Dissolution, *see* Noonan, J., "Papal Dissolution of Marriage: Fiction and Function."

Papal Reservations, *see* Lynch, J., "Some Landmarks in the Development of Papal Reservations up to 1400 A.D."

Parish, National, *see* Bevilacqua, A., "Problem Areas in Chancery Practice."

Pastoral Care, *see*

Ament, R., "People With Dignity: A Pastoral Program for the Divorced Catholic."

Farrell, W., "A Parish Plan for Ministry to Divorced Catholics."

Finnegan, J., "Marrige/Pastoral Care."

Kosnik, A., "The Pastoral Care of Those Involved in Canonically Invalid Marriages."

Pastoral Council, *see*

Morrissey, M., "Issues in Chancery Practice."

O'Meara, T., "Theological Reflections on Insitutional Renewal in the Church."

Pastoral Guide to Canon Law, The, see CLSA Committee on Continuing Education.

Pastoral Planning, *see*

Cain, J., "The Chancery in a Changing Church."

Dreher, J., "New Wineskins for New Wine. The Need for Pastoral Planning and Leadership Development for a Church in Transition."

Greeley, A., "A Social Organizational View of the Catholic Church."

Pastors, *see*

Janicki, J., "Limited Term of Office and Retirement."

Lopez, F., "Performance Evaluation for Pastors."

Patrimony, *see* O'Connor, D., et al., "Current Issues in Religious Law."

Paul VI, Pope, *see*

Morrisey, F., "The Spirit of Canon Law: Teachings of Pope Paul VI."

Sheets, J., "Ministry, Spirituality and the Canon Lawyer."

Pelikan, Jaroslav, "Law and Dogma: Some Historical Interrelations," '69 *Proceedings*, 69-77. (*Also, The Jurist*, 30 (1970) 133-144.)

There has been astonishingly little collaboration between these two fields, states the author. He offers some instances in which historical research into the development of doctrine is very much waiting for the application to its source materials of the methods and insights of the history of law, as, e.g., heresiology, the Nicene Creed, and the doctrine of atonement and *satisfactio*. Pelikan says that the outstanding instance of collaboration is the doctrine of the Trinity, a classic case of the development of doctrine not only on the basis of Scripture but also through the instrumentality of the *potestas jurisdictionis* and *jus circa sacra*. He hopes that in the years to come law and dogma may find their way closer to each other.

Penalties, *see*

Green, T., et al., "Report of the Special Committee of the Task Force of the Canon Law Society of America on the Proposed Schema *De Delictis et Poenis*."

Lynch, J., "The Limits of *Communio* in the Pre-Constantinian Church."

Provost, J., "Revision of Book V of the Code of Canon Law. Discussion of Tentative Draft."

Penance, *see*

Geary, P., "Civil Discovery and Confidentiality of Church Documents."

Green, T., et al., "Reflections on Other Parts of the Proposed Draft *De Sacramentis.*"

Pennington, M. Basil, "The Structure of the Section Concerning Religious Life in the Revised Code," *The Jurist,* 25 (1965) 271-290.

This paper was presented at the Eastern Regional Meeting at Hartford in 1965. The author views Vatican II's *De Ecclesia* (*Lumen Gentium*), chapter VI on "*De Religiosis,*" as offering the basic guidelines for structuring a new law for religious.

People of God, *see*

Bauer, N., "People of God Schema: Clerics—Function versus Call."

Green, T., "Reflections on the People of God Schema."

Kinney, J., "Rights and Duties of the Faithful in the Schema 'People of God': An Encourgement to Exercise Them."

Komonchak, J., "A New Law for the People of God: Some Theological Reflections."

McBrien, R., "A Preliminary Ecclesiological Statement."

Provost, J., "The People of God: Law or Politics?"

Sheehan, M., " 'Is There Any Life in the Church Beyond the Diocese?' Supra-Diocesan Structures and Church Governance."

Permanency, *see*

Brown, R. "Non-inclusion: A Form of Simulation."

See also Commitment, Permanent.

Permanent Deacon, *see* Deacon.

Permanent Seminar, *see* CLSA Permanent Seminar.

Perry, Joseph N., "Teenage Marriages: What The Church is Doing," *The Living Light,* 13 (1976) 553-559.

Policies and practices in over thirty dioceses in the U.S. and Canada were surveyed for what they are doing about teenage marriages and their tendency to end in divorce. In addition to marriage readiness assessment, Perry points to a need for catechesis and counseling. *See* CLSA Committee on Continuing Education.

Personality Disorders, *see*

Bauer, F., "Relative Incapacity to Establish a Christian Conjugal Union."

Graham, G., "Personality Disorders and Their Effect on the Validity of Marriage."

Keating, J.R., "Sociopathic Personality."

Russon, G.W., "The Assessment of Personality Disorder in Marriage."

Wrenn, L., *Annulments.*

Wrenn, L., *Decisions.*

Personality Test Data, *see* Swierzowski, S., et al., "The Use of Objective and Projective Personality Test Data in the Determination of Nullity of Marriages: A New Method."

Peter, Val J., "Problems of Agency and Moral Responsibility: A Practical Proposal," *Studia Canonica,* 11 (1977) 153-166.

This paper was presented at the Midwest Regional Meeting in 1977 and calls on the CLSA to produce a code of professional responsibility for each type of "agency."

Pfnausch, Edward, "Implications of Pre-Marital Preparation," '75 *Proceedings,* 84-93.

The author examines the informed preparation of a couple for marriage in the light of the fundamental right to marry. He explores a program for marriage preparation that involves a broad commitment on the part of the entire diocese.

Philadelphia, *see* CLSA, *Proceedings of the Thirty-Eighth Annual Convention,* Philadelphia, Pennsylvania, 1976.

Philosophy, *see*

Bourke, V., "The Analogy of Law."

Bourke, V., "Martial Fidelity and Philosophy."

Crosson, F., "Liberty and Authority in the Church."

Dupré, L. & C., "The Indissolubility of Christian Marriage and the Common Good."

Fontinell, E., "Authority and Freedom in the Christian Community, Expressed in the Structures of the Institution."

Westley, R., "The Problematic of Permanent Commitment."

Procedural Innovations, *see*

Provost, J., "Tribunal Future Shock: Alternatives for Justice."

Sanson, R., "Some Procedural Innovations: Legal? Healing?"

Schmidt, R., "Facilitating Tribunal Procedure."

Procedural Law, *see*

Dillon, E., "*De processibus*: An Analysis of Some Key Provisions."

Doyle, T., & Licari, R., " 'Everything You Ever Wanted to Know About the Competent Forum But Were Afraid to Ask.' "

Greeley, A., "Church Marriage Procedures and the Contemporary Family."

Green, T., "Procedural Law: Reflections on the Proposed Schema."

Morrisey, F., "The Current Status of Procedural Law."

Noonan, J., "Ursa's Case."

Wrenn, L., "Marriage—Indissoluble or Fragile?"

Procedure for the Selection of Bishops in the United States: A Suggested Implementation of Present Papal Norms, *see* CLSA Committee on the Selection of Bishops; CLSA Publications.

Proceedings of the Canon Law Society of America, *see* CLSA Publications.

Prohibition of Marriage, *see Vetitum.*

Promises, *see* Marriage Promises.

Providence, Diocese of, *see* Dreher, J., "New Wineskins for New Wine. The Need for Pastoral Planning and Leadership Development for a Church in Transition."

Provisional Plan for Choosing Bishops, see CLSA Committee on the Selection of Bishops.

Provost, James, et al., "What Role for Dispensed Priests?" *Origins*, v. 4, 491-496.

This is a report prepared for the National Federation of Priests' Councils by an *ad hoc* committee of the CLSA that included James Provost, Kenneth Lasch and Harmon Skillin. For its content *see* CLSA, "Dispensed Priests in Ecclesial Ministry: A Canonical Reflection," *Chicago Studies*, 14 (1975) 121-133.

"Revision of Book V of the Code of Canon Law. Discussion of Tentative Draft," *Studia Canonica*, 9 (1975) 135-152.

This paper was presented at the Eastern Regional Meeting at Worcester, Massachusetts in 1974. The author discusses the contents of the draft and the reactions to it by Canadian and American Canon Law Societies. Provost offers personal reflections on fundamental issues which remain to be faced before a final penal law can be genuinely termed a revision of Church law.

"Structuring the Church as a *Communio*," *The Jurist*, 36 (1976) 191-245.

The author presents an analysis of the social organization of the Church with application of this to various levels of realization of Church as a communion. He suggests a number of practical alternatives for those organizing and administering the Church today. *See* CLSA Permanent Seminar.

"Structuring the Community," *The Pastoral Guide to Canon Law*, 269-280.

Church structures from the parish through the universal level are reviewed in brief question and answer format. *See* CLSA Committee on Continuing Education.

"Tribunal Future Shock: Alternatives for Justice," '76 *Proceedings*, 118-122.

The author's thesis is that we are not irrevocably tied to the centralized tribunal. There are possible alternatives: circuit courts, district courts and the parish tribunal that can assist in our interim response to the growing rate of marital breakdown among Catholics, at least until the Christian community itself is ready to assume more responsibility in aiding those whose marriages do break down.

"True or False Reform in the Church?" *The Jurist*, 38 (1978) 257-267.

The author sees canon law as a key element in Church reform and he explores the reasons why there has been no response to the concerns of the CLSA regarding the renewal of canon law in the Church. This is a talk delivered as CLSA President at the Catholic University of America.

"Structuring the Church as *Missio*," *The Jurist*, 39 (1979) 220-288.

The author considers the long-range implications of the insights arrived at in this study of Church as Mission. He builds a vision of Church organized, programmed and evaluated on *missio* principles. The official structures of the Church are presented as empowerments for individuals and groups to actualize the *missio* reality of Church. *See* CLSA Permanent Seminar.

"The People of God: Law or Politics?" '80 *Proceedings*, 44-59.

Various questions canon lawyers will have to face when implementing the new Code are sketched.

Prusak, Bernard, "Hospitality Extended or Denied: *Koinōnia* Incarnate from Jesus to Augustine," *The Jurist,* 36 (1976) 89-126.

The author examines the various stages of expressing communion moving from table hospitality through questions affecting the unity of faith to a development of communion of bishops as expressing the communion of communities. *See* CLSA Permanent Seminar.

Psychology, *see*

Gill, J., "Psychological Impact of the Change to Optional Celibacy."

Higgins, J., "Psychological Influences on the Marriage Bond."

Kennedy, E., "Signs of Life in Marriage."

Psychoneurotic Interpersonal Reaction, *see* Braceland, R., "Psychoneurotic Interpersonal Reaction: Incompatibility and the Tribunal."

-R-

Read, Dennis, A review of W. Bassett's *The Bond of Marriage: An Ecumenical and Interdisciplinary Study, The Jurist,* 29 (1969) 104-108.

Recent Roman Replies, see Biechler, J., ed.; Surges, E., ed.

Regan, Columkille, "The Schema of Canons on Institutes of Life Consecrated by Profession of the Evangelical Counsels," '77 *Proceedings,* 98-111.

This is a CLSA Task Force evaluation of the canons.

Regin, Douglas, "Overview of Diocesan Regulation of Adolescent Marriage Since Vatican II," *Marriage Studies I,* 25-37.

The guidelines of forty-six dioceses are reviewed, and a chart describes the details of each so they can be compared to one another.

Reh, Francis, "A Bishop Looks at the CLSA," '70 *Proceedings,* 60-61.

Reich, Warren, *see* Farley, L. & Reich, W., "Toward 'An Immediate Internal Forum Solution' for Deserving Couples in Canonically Insoluble Marriage Cases," *The Jurist,* 30 (1970) 45-74.

Reinhardt, Marion, A review of A. Maida's *The Tribunal Reporter, The Jurist,* 30 (1970) 404-408.

"Error Qualitatis in Errorem Personae Redundans," '73 *Proceedings*, 55-69.

A study of error in the classical canonists and others and in recent Rotal jurisprudence leads the author to conclude that this area of error is open to a development of jurisprudence. Reinhardt says that the old law is not precise either from the style and practice of the Roman curia, or from the common and constant practice of learned men. He believes that we can follow Thomas Aquinas and declare a marriage invalid when there is an error about a quality that is directly and principally intended for then it redounds into an error of person.

"Relationships with the Roman Dicasteries," '79 *Proceedings*, 83-90.

The author brings his own extensive experience to a practical exchange of views on how to better relationships between Tribunals and Roman offices.

Relative Incapacity, *see* Incapacity, Relative.

Relativism, Historical, *see* Meyendorff, J., "Historical Relativism and Authority in Christian Dogma."

Religious, *see* Institutes of Life.

Religious Educators

Cargill, J., "Understanding the One-Parent Child in the Classroom."

Dunning, J., "Two Fly Into the Lovebird's Nest, Or Catechesis for Building the Covenant."

Young, J., "The Religious Educator and the Children of Divorce."

Renewal, *see*

Brundage, J., "The Creative Canonist: His Role in Church Reform."

Gumbleton, T., "The Diocesan Synod of Detroit: Renewal in Process."

O'Meara, T., "Theological Reflections on Institutional Renewal in the Church."

Orsy, L., "The Dynamic Spirit of Common Law and the Renewal of Canon Law."

Renewal Through Community and Experimentation, see CLSA Workshop on *Community Life and Experimentation*; O'Rourke, K., ed.

Roman Rota, *see*

Brown, R., "The Development of Local Jurisprudence."

Burns, D., "Moral Certitude."

Cunningham, R., "Recent Rotal Decisions and Today's Marriage Theology: Nothing Has Changed—Or Has It?"

Keating, J.R., "Sociopathic Personality."

Lavin, M., "The Rotal Decision Before Serrano, April 5, 1973: Some Observations Concerning Jurisprudence, Procedure and Risk."

Wrenn, L., *Decisions*.

Rotal Decisions. The CLSA has made available for the private use of CLSA members a number of Rotal decisions translated into English by James McEnerny, William Cogan, Joseph Persich and Gerald Costello.

Russon, G.W., "The Assessment of Personality Disorder in Marriage," *Studia Canonica*, 9 (1975) 57-61.

This paper was presented at the Northwest Regional Meeting at Cochrane, Alberta, Canada in 1975. (The region combines CLSA members from the Northwestern United States and Western Canadian members of the Canadian Canon Law Society.) The author discusses various problems connected with making an assessment of this nature.

Ryan, J. Joseph, "Canon Law in the Gregorian Reform Epoch (c. 1050-1125): Historical Perspectives in the Present Age of Renewal," *Law for Liberty*, 38-51.

Ryan presents the eleventh century as a turning point, and sees several key developments of the reform: strengthening the Roman See; use of ancient Church law as a basis for reform; the influence of the Pseudo-Isidore; and practical concerns relative to reform, reunion and reconquests. *See* CLSA Symposia, *The Role of Law in the Church*.

Ryan, Richard, "The Dispensing Authority of the Residential Bishop," '77 *Proceedings*, 53-62.

The author demonstrates the significance of article 8b of Vatican II's *Christus Dominus* by offering a study of the foundation of the authority of the residential Bishop, its limits of pre-emption, the authority to dispense from the general laws of the Church, the relationship of Canon 81 to article 8b and those laws reserved by the Pope in *De Episcoporum Muneribus*.

-S-

Sacraments and Law, *see*

Green, T., et al., "Reflections on Other Parts of the Proposed Draft *De Sacramentis.*"

Green, T., et al., "Report of a Special Committee of the Task Force of the Canon Law Society of America on the Marriage Canons of the Proposed *Schema Documenti Pontificii quo Disciplina Canonica de Sacramentis Recognoscitur.*"

Green, T., et al., "Sacramental Law: Reflections on the Proposed Schema."

Sacraments, Right to the, *see*

Buckley, F., "The Right to the Sacraments of Initiation."

See also Eucharist, The Rights of the Invalidly Married to; Marriage, Canonical Bases for Deferral or Refusal of.

St. Louis, *see* CLSA, *Proceedings of the Fortieth Annual Convention*, St. Louis, Missouri, 1978.

St. Paul, *see* CLSA, *Proceedings of the Thirty-Sixth Annual Convention*, St. Paul, Minnesota, 1974.

Sanchez, Robert, "The Early Republic's Challenge to Catholic Church Governance: Bicentennial Reflctions of an American Canonist: A Response," '76 *Proceedings*, 19-23.

In response to a talk by Robert Kennedy, the author distinguishes between external and internal structures of the Church. He recognizes that the Church has something to learn from the American concept of Federalism—its success and its failures—but he calls attention to the 19th chapter of Matthew and says that the challenge of the Church today consists in our faithfulness to the Gospel of Jesus Christ.

San Diego, *see* CLSA, *Proceedings of the Thirty—Seventh Annual Convention*, San Diego, California, 1975.

Sanson, Robert, "Some Procedural Innovations: Legal? Healing?" '78 *Proceedings*, 101-108.

The author examines the practice of adapting procedures and using "ordinary means" in the light of legality, practicality and pastoral benefit. He says that the procedural medium must be the pastoral message.

Schema, Proposed, *see* Code, Proposed New.

Schmemann, Alexander, "The Indissolubility of Marriage: The Theological Tradition of the East," *The Bond of Marriage*, 97-105.

The Eastern Orthodox approach to marriage is explained in terms of liturgy and *theoria. See* CLSA Symposia, *The Bond of Marriage.*

Schmidt, Ronald, "Facilitating Tribunal Procedure," '76 *Proceedings*, 74-91.

This seminar reports on the findings of a survey of 32 diocesan tribunals which handle a large volume of cases. The author offers practical suggestions for facilitating Tribunal practice together with sample forms.

See Buckley, J. & Schmidt, R., "Experience and Possibilities of Canonical Legal Aid."

Schoenherr, Richard A., "Holy Power? Holy Authority? And Holy Celibacy?" *Celibacy in the Church*, 126-142.

Sociologist Schoenherr puts the question of celibacy as it is raised in modern times in the context of authority, and the issues around authority and power in the Church. *See* CLSA Symposia, *The Future Discipline of Priestly Celibacy.*

Schumacher, William, et al., *Matrimonial Jurisprudence, United States, 1973*, Toledo, OH, CLSA, 1975.

Scripture and Canon Law, *see*

Ahern, B., "Law and the Gospel."

Crossan, D., "Divorce and Remarriage in the New Testament."

MacRae, G., "Freedoms and Rights of the Christian: New Testament Foundations."

MacRae, G., "New Testament Perspectives on Divorce and Remarriage."

Murphy, T., "Towards a Theology of Marriage."

O'Meara, T., "The Nature, Extent and Style of Authority in the Church."

Shepherd, M., "The Rights of the Baptized."

Sloyan, G., "Biblical and Patristic Motives for Celibacy of Church Ministers."

Stanley, D., "Discerning the Permanent and Transitory: The Experience of the Apostolic Church."

See also New Testament.

Seattle, see CLSA, *Proceedings of the Thirty-Fourth Annual Convention,* Seattle, Washington, 1972.

Selected Passages from Religious Constitutions Dealing with the Evangelical Counsels and Community Life, see Boyle, P., ed.

Serrano, Joseph, *see* Lavin, M., "The Rotal Decision Before Serrano, April 5, 1973: Some Observations Concerning Jurisprudence, Procedure, and Risk."

Sexism and Church Law: Equal Rights and Affirmative Action, see CLSA Symposia, *Women and Church Law*; Coriden, J., ed.

Sexton, William, "A Comparative Examination of the Exercise of Authority in the Church," '71 *Proceedings*, 42-54.

The author, a social scientist, analyzes bureaucratic structuring.

Sheehan, Michael J., " 'Is There Any Life in the Church Beyond the Diocese?' Supra-Diocesan Structures and Church Governance in Book II, the People of God," '80 *Proceedings*, 132-150.

The place of episcopal conferences in the new law and their relationship to other structures is evaluated. Two appendices are given, the second one developed by Daniel Hoye analyzing the references to the Conference of Bishops in the pre-1980 drafts for the new Code.

Sheets, John, "Ministry, Spirituality and the Canon Lawyer," *Studia Canonica*, 12 (1978) 57-71.

Drawing on the characteristic spirituality of priests (and of all Christians) and the nature and mission of canon lawyers (based on the address of Pope Paul VI to the International Congress of Canon Law at Rome in 1977), the author offers the characteristics of spirituality proper to the ministry of canon lawyers. This was an address to the Midwest Regional meeting in 1977.

Shepherd, Massey, H., "The Rights of the Bapitzed," *The Case for Freedom: Human Rights in the Church*, 33-45.

Exploring the New Testament concepts of new life and *exousia*, Shepherd urges a deeper theological awareness of the role of the Christian in the world. *See* CLSA Symposia, *Rights in the Church.*

Simulation, *see* Brown, R., "Non-inclusion: A Form of Simulation."

Simplification of Procedures in Privilege of Faith and Lack of Form Cases, see CLSA Publications.

Sin and Law, *see* Curran, C., "Law and Conscience in the Christian Context."

Skillin, Harmon, *see* CLSA, "Dispensed Priests in Ecclesial Ministry: A Canonical Reflection."

Sloyan, Gerard, "Biblical and Patristic Motives for Celibacy of Church Ministers," *Celibacy in the Church*, 13-29.

> Working mainly with patristic sources, Sloyan demonstrates the early discipline on celibacy is rooted in an attitude in the Church which was unsympathetic to sex and to marriage. *See* CLSA Symposia, *The Future Discipline of Priestly Celibacy.*

Sociology, *see*

Conroy, D., "The Statistics and Crisis of Divorce."

Greeley, A., "Church Marriage Procedures and the Contemporary Family."

Greeley, A., "Leadership and Friendship: A Sociologist's Viewpoint."

Greeley, A., "A Social Organizational View of the Catholic Church."

McDaniel, H., "A Social Agency Looks at the Family."

O'Dea, T., "Authority and Freedom in the Church: Tension, Balance and Contradiction, An Historico-Sociological View."

Schoenherr, R., "Holy Power? Holy Authority? And Holy Celibacy?"

Sexton, W., "A Comparative Examination of the Exercise of Authority in the Church."

Sussman, M., "The Family in the 1960's: Facts, Fictions, Problems, Prospects and Institutional Linkages."

Warwick, D., "Personal and Organizational Effectiveness in the Roman Catholic Church."

Sociopathic Personality, *see* Keating, J.R., "Sociopathic Personality."

Spanish Speaking People, *see* Elizondo, V., "The Spanish Speaking and the Law."

Spirituality, *see* Sheets, J., "Ministry, Spirituality and the Canon Lawyer."

Stanley, David, "Discerning the Permanent and Transitory: The Experience of the Apostolic Church," *Law for Liberty*, 19-27.

> From the New Testament perspective, this position paper contrasts the

forms, methods and structures which are inherent and perennial in the Church, and those which are borrowed and adapted from cultural situations and therefore more transitory. *See* CLSA Symposia, *The Role of Law in the Church.*

Stern, Robert L., "How Priests came to be Celibate: An Oversimplification," *Celibacy in the Church,* 76-83.

Stern traces the discipline on celibacy to a spiritual concern, rooted in the ascetic life of religious clergy and gradually applied to all priests. *See* CLSA Symposia, *The Future Discipline of Priestly Celibacy.*

Stocker, Thomas, et al., *Matrimonial Jurisprudence, United States, 1974,* Toledo, OH, CLSA, 1976.

Matrimonial Jurisprudence, United States, 1975-1976, Toledo, OH, CLSA, 1977.

Stringfellow, William, "The Law, the Church and the Needs of Society," '70 *Proceedings,* 47-52.

The author discusses the cases of Fathers Daniel and Philip Berrigan and their witness in the light of I Peter 2:9-10, 13-17, whereby, in the words of Stingfellow, they chose to "honor the emperor" by becoming "fugatives from injustice . . . powerless criminals in a day of criminal power."

Subsidiarity, Principle of, *see*

Bassett, W., "Subsidiarity, Order and Freedom in the Church."

CLSA Symposia, *Unity and Subsidiarity in the Church: Rome and the Conference of Bishops.*

Goedert, R., "Selection of Bishops. A Canonical and Pastoral Critique of the New Norms."

Green, T., "Reflections on the People of God Schema."

McNally, R., "The Roman Process of Martin Luther: A Failure in Subsidiarity."

O'Rourke, K., "The New Instruction on Formation of Religious."

Surges, Edward, ed., *Recent Roman Replies,* Hartford, CT, CLSA, 1967.

Sussman, Marvin B., "The Family in the 1960's: Facts, Fictions, Problems, Prospects and Institutional Linkages," *The Bond of Marriage,* 223-246.

Statistical information about families is analyzed with a view toward developing theoretical understandings of changes now taking place, from a social scientist's point of view. *See* CLSA Symposia, *The Bond of Marriage.*

Swierzowski, Stanislaus, et al., "The Use of Objective and Projective Personality Test Data in the Determination of Nullity of Marriages: A New Method," '75 *Proceedings*, 106-128.

In an actual case study, the Albany Tribunal demonstrates how utilizing the Minnesota Multiphasic Personality Inventory, the Edwards Personal Preference Schedule, the Projective Sentence Completion Test, and Projective Figure Drawings, an overall personality description can be abstracted for each party as well as a description of the manner in which two such personalities would be likely to interact in a marital relationship.

Swift, Thomas, "The Human Dimensions of Authority and Obedience in a Faith Community," '71 *Proceedings*, 28-41.

The author offers two modes of thinking about authority-obedience. He discusses the process from which authority-obedience arise, juridical authority, the ambivalence of authority-obedience relationship as expressed in law, the relation of internal freedom and response to external authority or law. He hopes to clarify what nature and grace have to build on in the realm of authority and obedience. Swift suggests several emphases for future structures of authority and obedience that develop through the free and informed cooperation of those involved.

Synod, *see* Detroit, Archdiocese of.

Synods, Episcopal, *see* Episcopal Synods.

-T-

Teaching Canon Law, *see* Canon Law, Teaching.

Team Ministry, *see* Coriden, J., & Mangan, M., "Team Ministry."

Teenage Marriages, *see* Marriage, Teenage.

Theology, *see*

Alesandro, J., "The Revision of Church Law: Conflict and Reconciliation."

Brunett, A., "The Diocesan Synod of Detroit: The Theology Underlying the Synod Document."

Burghardt, W., "Church Structure: A Theologian Reflects on History."

Curran, C., "Law and Conscience in the Christian Context."

Curran, C., "Responsibility in Moral Theology: Centrality, Foundations, and Implications for Ecclesiology."

Green, T., "Reflections on the People of God Schema."

Green, T., et al., "Reflections on Other Parts of the Proposed Draft *De Sacramentis.*"

Hess, H., "Ecclesial Rights in the Early Christian Community: A Theological Study."

Himes, M., "The Current State of Sacramental Theology as a Background to the New Code."

Hynous, D., "Theology of Participative Leadership."

Jegen, C., "Theological Consideration on the Problematic of Permanent Commitment."

Komonchak, J., "A New Law for the People of God: Some Theological Reflections."

Lonergan, B., "The Transition from a Classicist World-View to Historical Mindedness."

Meyer, B., "The Perennial Problem of the Church: Institutional Change."

Meyer, C., "Christian Freedom."

Molloy, T., "The Theological Foundation of Ecclesiastical Due Process.

Morrisey, F., "The Spirit of Canon Law: Teaching of Pope Paul VI."

O'Meara, T., "Theological Reflections on Institutional Renewal in the Church."

Padovano, A., "A Theology of Church Government."

Shepherd, M., "The Rights of the Baptized."

See also Marriage, Theology of.

Think Tank, *see* CLSA Think Tank.

Thomas, Barbara, "Participative Leadership in Religious Life," '72 *Proceedings*, 86-97.

In the light of changing governmental structures, the author reflects on the efforts of her own community to provide for participative leadership. A lengthy discussion and question and answer session follow.

"Models of Governance for Religious," '76 *Proceedings*, 92-98.

This seminar is a study of structures, from the bureaucratic structure of the past to the participative (or relational) structure to which religious communities were called by Vatican II. Thomas concludes with a call for a still newer and more creative structure, the "collaborative."

Thomas, Milton, "An Analysis and Critique of Marriage Preparation Programs," *Marriage Studies I,* 1-24.

The formation of EFM (Education for Marriage) is described as well as the development and use of PREPARE, a computerized instrument for evaluating readiness for marriage.

Thrasher, Robert W., "Reflections on Canon 1014," *Marriage Studies I,* 144-155.

The presumption in favor of marriage is explored with a view to possible changes both in the proposed revision of the Code and in light of internal forum solutions.

Tierney, Brian, "Roots of Western Constitutionalism in the Church's Own Tradition: The Significance of the Council of Constance," *We, the People of God . . . ,* 113-128.

Analyzing the decree *Haec Sancta* of the Council of Constance, Tierney sets it in its historical perspective and outlines some of the debate which has followed. He points to some modern implications in terms of collegiality and constitutionalism. *See* CLSA Symposia, *A Constitution for the Church.*

Tradition, *see*

Cardman, F., "Tradition, Hermeneutics and Ordination."

Kennedy, R., "Canonical Tradition and Christian Rights."

Schmemann, A., "The Indissolubility of Marriage: The Theological Tradition of the East."

Tribunal, *see*

Braceland, F., "Psychoneurotic Interpersonal Reaction: Incompatibility and the Tribunal."

Burns, D., "Procedure in Second Instance Courts."

Burns, D., et al., "Report of Committee for Tribunal Assistance."

Catoir, J., "An Analysis of the Evolution of Tribunal Practice."

CLSA, Committee on Alternatives to Tribunal Procedures.

CLSA, Committee on Tribunal Decision Making.

CLSA Publications, *Audio-Visual Learning on Marriage, Divorce, Tribunal Practice.*

CLSA Publications, *Matrimonial Jurisprudence, United States.*

Dillon, E., "*De processibus*: An Analysis of Some Key Provisions."

Doyle, T., & Licari, R., " 'Everything You Ever Wanted to Know About the Competent Forum But Were Afraid to Ask.' "

Geary, P., "Civil Discovery and Confidentiality of Church Documents."

Green, T., "*Causas Matrimoniales* and the A.P.N.—A Survey."

Häring, B., "A Theological Appraisal of Marriage Tribunals."

LaDue, W., "*Causas Matrimoniales* and the American Procedural Norms —A Comparison."

Logar, W., "Liberty and Justice for All: An Ecclesial Interpretation."

Logar, W., "Minorities Before the Law."

Lucas, J., "The Role of the Tribunal in Second Marriages: The Prohibition."

Maida, A., ed., *The Tribunal Reporter.*

McDevitt, A., "Report of Committee on Alternatives to Tribunal Procedures."

O'Callaghan, M., et al, "Committee Report on Regional Tribunals."

Provost, J., "Tribunal Future Shock: Alternatives for Justice."

Reinhardt, M., "Relationships with the Roman Dicasteries."

Sanson, R., "Some Procedural Innovations: Legal? Healing?"

Schmidt, R., "Facilitating Tribunal Procedure."

Wrenn, L., *Annulments.*

Wrenn, L., *Decisions.*

Wrenn, L., "Marriage—Indissoluble or Fragile?"

Tribunal Reporter, The, see Maida, A., ed.

Tridentine Church, *see* McNally, R., "The Tridentine Church: A Study in Ecclesiology."

Trisco, Robert F., "The Variety of Procedures in Modern History," *The Choosing of Bishops*, 33-60.

Procedures for selection of bishops which have been in effect since the beginning of the nineteenth century in various parts of the world are reviewed. *See* CLSA Committee on the Selection of Bishops.

Trullo Cases, see CLSA Publications.

-U-

Unity, *see* CLSA Symposia, *Unity and Subsidiarity in the Church: Rome and the Conference of Bishops.,*

Ursa, *see* Noonan, J., "Ursa's Case."

-V-

van der Poel, Cornelius, "Marriage and Family as Expressions of *Communio* in the Church," *The Jurist,* 36 (1976) 59-88.

The author explores the interpersonal relationships which signify and develop the ecclesial realities of community and communion. He says that promoting this relationship in a communion of life and dealing with its failure are primary pastoral concerns for the Church. Van der Poel shows how the communion model of Church can contribute to the practical living of Christian faith. *See* CLSA Permanent Seminar.

"Influences of an 'Annulment Mentality,' " *The Jurist,* 40 (1980) 384-399.

In this revised version of a presentation to the Eastern Regional Canon Law meeting at Hershey, Pennsylvania in 1978, van der Poel suggests that an "Annulment Mentality" may indeed be present among Catholics in the United States, but he argues this does not arise from the practices of tribunals but from the cultural and moral atmosphere within the country itself.

Vatican Documents, *see* Foley, N., "Women in Vatican Documents 1960 to the Present."

Vazquez, Lucy, "Report of Committee on the Status of Women in the Church," '75 *Proceedings,* 185-192. (*Also, Origins,* v. 5, 260-264.)

This committee demonstrates how the inequality of women in the Church is challenged today by Society, by other Christian churches and religious denominations, and even within the Roman Catholic Church itself.

Vetitum, see

Bevilacqua, A., "Problem Areas in Chancery Practice."

Lucas, J., "The Role of the Tribunal in Second Marriages: The Prohibition."

Natale, S., "The Tribunal *Vetitum*: Limit Setting and Confrontation."

Voegtle, Leonard, "Report on Religious Seminar," '71 *Proceedings*, 62-64.
This seminar briefly outlines the major areas of concern in contemporary religious life.

-W-

Warwick, Donald P., "Personal and Organizational Effectiveness in the Roman Catholic Church," *We, the People of God . . .* , 91-110.
Using social science insights into organizational effectiveness, Warwick analyzes the structures of authority, leadership and law, the central administration of the Church, the role of clergy, and the role of lay persons in the Church. *See* CLSA Symposia, *A Constitution for the Church.*

"Human Freedom and the Church of the Future," *The Case for Freedom: Human Rights in the Church*, 107-128.
The meaning of human freedom and its contemporary setting are explored, with suggestions for environmental freedom, dispositional freedom, and developmental freedom in the Church of the future. *See* CLSA Symposia, *Rights in the Church.*

Washington, *see* CLSA, *Proceedings of the Thirty-Fifth Annual Convention*, Washington, D.C. 1973.

Washington Nineteen, *see* Buckley, J. & Schmidt, R., "Experience and Possibilities of Canonical Legal Aid."

We, the People of God . . . A Study of Constitutional Government for the Church, see CLSA Symposia, *A Constitution for the Church*; Coriden, J., ed.

Westley, Richard, "The Problematic of Permanent Commitment," '70 *Proceedings*, 71-79.
The author offers a philosophical approach to permanent commitment.

He raises a number of questions about the philosophical justification of keeping promises or taking vows and presents a diagnosis of the current situation. This workshop was given in connection with the workshop of Carol Jegen (q.v.).

Whelan, Charles M., "Problems of Drafting a Bill of Rights for the Church," *The Case for Freedom: Human Rights in the Church*, 165-170.

Procedural and content problems are explored as a result of discussions during this CLSA symposium. *See* CLSA Symposia, *Rights in the Church.*

Who Decides for the Church?, *see* CLSA Symposia, *Co-responsibility in the Church*; Coriden, J., ed.

Wojnar, Meletius M., "Participation of the Clergy and Laity in the Election of Bishops According to the Discipline of the Oriental Catholic Churches," *The Choosing of Bishops*, 61-73.

Although the tradition since at least Justinian has been for clergy below the level of bishop and lay persons not to have an active voice in the election of bishops, they did have a role in surfacing candidates and suggesting individual names. The fate of this tradition in modern times is discussed for the Armenian, Chaldean, Rumanian, Melkite, Syrian and Coptic churches in union with Rome. *See* CLSA Committee on the Selection of Bishops.

Women, *see*

Bevilacqua, A., ed., *The ERA in Debate: What Can It Mean for Church Law?*

Bissonnette, R., "Ecclesiastical Ministry and Women."

Brennan, M., "Standing in Experience: A Reflection on the Status of Women in the Church."

CLSA Symposia, *Women and Church Law.*

Green, T., "Reflections on the People of God Schema."

Vazquez, L., "Report of Committee on the Status of Women in the Church."

Women Religious, *see* Institutes of Life.

Worship, *see* Jegen, C., "Worship and *Missio.*"

Wrenn, Lawrence, ed., *Common Sources of Nullity*, Hartford, CT, CLSA, 1968.

Annulments, Hartford, CT, CLSA, 1970; 2nd ed. 1972; 3rd ed., Toledo, OH, CLSA, 1978.

This work is a reference manual intended principally for tribunal personnnel and for parish priests, seminarians and others who wish to acquaint themselves with the jurisprudence on marriage. In addition to a selective bibliography and chapters that discuss the meaning of jurisprudence, the American Procedural Norms, *Causas Matrimoniales*, moral certitude, etc., both the traditional grounds (e.g., impotence, simulation, force and fear, etc.) and the newer grounds (e.g., lack of due competence or of due discretion and associated disorders) are defined and explained in some detail.

ed., *Divorce and Remarriage in the Catholic Church*, New York, NY, Newman, 1973.

This work is the result of a project initiated by the CLSA. Ten scholars from various fields consider the Tribunal system of the Catholic Church. *See* CLSA Committee on Tribunal Decision Making. For a review of this work, *see* Morrisey, F., *Studia Canonica*, 7 (1973) 320-321.

"Marriage—Indissoluble or Fragile?" *Divorce and Remarriage in the Catholic Church*, 134-149.

In light of the various studies by the ad hoc committee he directed, Wrenn raises several questions concerning the Church's understanding of indissolubility and suggests it amounts to recognizing the fragility of marriage.

Decisions, Toledo, OH, CLSA, 1980.

This volume is a companion to *Annulments*. Thirty-two actual cases (using fictional names and places) on a variety of grounds are presented in the traditional manner, viz., by offering the facts, the law and the argument. There are translations of excerpts from Rotal decisions as well as current diagnostic criteria for the various personality disorders that may affect the validity of a marriage.

Wynn, John C., "Prevailing and Countervailing Trends in the Non-Catholic Churches," *Divorce and Remarriage in the Catholic Church*, 65-88.

The positions taken toward divorce and remarriage by various mainline Protestant churches, the Orthodox church, and Evangelical church movements are reviewed.

-Y-

Young, James J., "The Religious Educator and the Children of Divorce," *The Living Light*, 13 (1976) 588-598.

Noting the increasing number of children of divorce in Catholic parishes and schools, suggestions are made toward pastoral and educational sensitivity on behalf of these children. *See* CLSA, Committee on Continuing Education.

-Z-

Zizola, Giancarlo, "The Reformed Roman Curia," *We, the People of God . . .* , 49-77.

The reform of the Roman Curia by Paul VI is explained in detail with criticisms of elements which remain yet to be reformed. *See* CLSA Symposia, *A Constitution for the Church.*

APPENDIX

Presidents of the Canon Law Society of America, 1965-1980

1964-1965	Paul M. Boyle, C.P.
1965-1966	Peter J. Shannon
1966-1967	Alan McCoy, O.F.M.
1967-1968	Thomas J. Lynch
1968-1969	Adam J. Maida
1969-1970	Henry G. Bowen
1970-1971	Robert T. Kennedy
1971-1972	Raymond E. Goedert
1972-1974	Donald E. Heintschel
1974-1975	John T. Finnegan
1975-1976	Bertram F. Griffin
1976-1977	Edward J. Dillon
1977-1978	James H. Provost
1978-1979	John A. Alesandro
1979-1980	Dennis J. Burns
1980-1981	Richard A. Hill, S.J.

Executive-Coordinators of the Canon Law Society of America, 1965-1980

1965-1968	Paul M. Boyle, C.P.
1968-1974	Thomas J. Lynch
1974-1980	Donald E. Heintschel
1980-	James H. Provost